Collins Primary Maths ⑤
Homework Copymasters

Series Editor: Peter Clarke

Authors: Andrew Edmondson, Elizabeth Jurgensen,
Jeanette Mumford, Sandra Roberts

Contents

HCM	Title	Objective	Term/Week/Lesson
1	Snake sum game	To multiply and divide any positive integer up to 10 000 by 10 or 100 and understand the effect.	Au 1, 2
2	Revising multiplication facts	To know by heart all multiplication facts up to 10 × 10.	Au 2, 1
3	Revising multiplication and and division	To derive quickly or continue to derive quickly division facts corresponding to tables up to 10 × 10.	Au 2, 2
4	Doubling and halving	To use doubling or halving, starting from known facts. For example: double/halve any two-digit number by doubling/halving the tens first.	Au 3, 2
5	Helpful doubles	To use doubling or halving, starting from known facts. For example: find the ×16 table facts by doubling the ×8 table.	Au 3, 4
6	Wall fractions	To recognise when two simple fractions are equivalent.	Au 4, 2
7	Decimals in order	To know what each digit represents in a number with up to two decimal places.	Au 4, 4
8	Percentages	To begin to understand percentage as the number of parts in every 100.	Au 5, 1
9	Ratio problems	To solve simple problems using ideas of ratio and proportion.	Au 5, 4
10	Bat bar line charts	To solve a problem by representing and interpreting data in tables, charts, graphs and diagrams, including those generated by computer, for example: bar line charts, vertical axis labelled in 10s.	Au 6, 3
11	Calculating clothes costs	To develop calculator skills and use a calculator effectively.	Au 7, 2
12	Flexing rectangles	To solve mathematical problems or puzzles, recognise and explain patterns and relationships, generalise and predict. Suggest extensions asking "What if…?"	Au 8, 2
13	Folding triangles	To classify triangles (isosceles, equilateral, scalene), using criteria such as equal sides, equal angles, lines of symmetry.	Au 8, 4
14	Plotting shapes	To read and plot co-ordinates in the first quadrant.	Au 9, 2
15	Chessboard perimeters	To understand, measure and calculate perimeters of rectangles and regular polygons.	Au 9, 4
16	Measuring money	To record estimates and readings from readings from scales to a suitable degree of accuracy.	Au 10, 3
17	TV times	To use units of time: read the time on a 24-hour digital clock and use 24-hour clock notation, such as 19:53.	Au 10, 4
18	Adding up in the air	To use informal pencil and paper methods to support, record or explain additions.	Au 11, 2
19	In the playground	To use all four operations to solve simple word problems involving numbers and quantities based on "real life", using one or more steps.	Au 11, 4
20	Number sequences	To recognise and extend number sequences formed by counting from any number in steps of constant size, extending beyond zero when counting back.	Au 12, 1
21	Square numbers	To know squares of numbers to at least 10 × 10.	Au 12, 2

22	Spot the pairs	To multiply and divide any positive integer up to 10 000 by 10 or 100 and understand the effect.	Sp 1, 2
23	Facts reminder	To derive quickly or continue to derive quickly division facts corresponding to tables up to 10 × 10.	Sp 2, 1
24	Terrific 20s treasure hunt	To use closely related facts (e.g. multiply by 19 or 21 by multiplying by 20 and adjusting).	Sp 2, 5
25	Recording division	To extend written methods to short division of HTU by U.	Sp 3, 2
26	Holiday money	To use all four operations to solve simple word problems involving numbers and quantities based on "real life" and money, using one or more steps, including making simple conversions of pounds to foreign currency.	Sp 3, 4
27	Fraction pairs game	To relate fractions to division, and then use division to find simple fractions, including tenths and hundredths of numbers and quantities.	Sp 4, 2
28	Decimal pathways	To order a set of numbers or measurements with the same number of decimal places.	Sp 4, 4
29	Open cubes	To visualise 3D shapes from 2D drawings and identify different nets for an open cube.	Sp 5, 2
30	Dazzling diagonals	To solve mathematical problems or puzzles recognise and explain patterns and relationships, generalise and predict. Suggest extensions asking "What if…?"	Sp 5, 4
31	Star patterns	To make patterns from rotating shapes.	Sp 6, 3
32	Finding the square units	To understand and use the formula in words units "length × breadth" for the area of a rectangle.	Sp 7, 2
33	Choosing chocolates	To use, read and write standard metric units	Sp 7, 4
34	Packaging weights	To choose and use appropriate number operations to solve problems, and appropriate ways of calculating: mental, mental with jottings, written methods, calculator.	Sp 8, 2
35	Pencil pack graphs	To solve a problem by representing and interpreting data in tables, charts, graphs and diagrams, including those generated by a computer, for example: bar line charts, where intermediate points may have meaning (e.g. room temperature over time).	Sp 8, 4
36	Near multiples magic	To add or subtract the nearest multiple of 10 or 100, then adjust.	Sp 9, 2
37	Decimal tens game	To derive quickly, or continue to derive quickly all decimals that total 1.	Sp 9, 4
38	Shopping decimals	To extend written methods to addition of a pair of decimal fractions, both with one or both with two decimal places.	Sp 10, 2
39	Park problems	To use addition and subtraction to solve simple word problems involving numbers and quantities based on "real life" and money, using one or more steps.	Sp 10, 4
40	Look out for 25s	To recognise and extend number sequences.	Sp 11, 1
41	Making many multiples	To recognise multiples of 6, 7, 8, 9 up to 10.	Sp 11, 2
42	Estimates, estimates	To use the vocabulary of estimation and approximation.	Su 1, 2
43	Multiplication and division facts	To derive quickly, or continue to derive quickly division facts corresponding to tables up to 10 × 10.	Su 2, 1

Collins Primary Maths © HarperCollins*Publishers* Ltd 2000

44	Multiplication and division	To use known facts and place value to multiply and divide mentally.	Su 2, 5
45	Multiplication methods	To know by heart all multiplication facts up to 10 × 10.	Su 3, 2
46	More multiplication methods	To know by heart all multiplication facts up to 10 × 10.	Su 3, 3
47	Decimal jumps	To order a set of numbers or measurements with the same number of decimal places.	Su 4, 1
48	Fraction and decimal dominoes	To relate fractions to their decimal representations: that is, recognise the equivalence between the decimal and fraction forms of one half, one quarter, three quarters…tenths and hundredths.	Su 4, 4
49	Four in a row	To begin to understand percentage as the number of parts in every 100.	Su 5, 2
50	How many?	To solve simple problems using ideas of ratio and proportion.	Su 5, 4
51	Ranges	To calculate the range of a set of data.	Su 6, 3
52	Sports costs	To develop calculator skills and use a calculator effectively.	Su 7, 1
53	Four-square designs	To complete symmetrical patterns with two lines of symmetry at right angles (using squared paper or a pegboard).	Su 8, 2
54	Making a Rangoli pattern	To complete symmetrical patterns with two lines of symmetry at right angles (using squared paper or a pegboard).	Su 8, 4
55	Translation patterns	To recognise where a shape will be after a translation.	Su 9, 1
56	My birth day	To know and use the relationship between units of time.	Su 9, 4
57	Everyday estimating	To suggest suitable units and measuring equipment to estimate or measure capacity.	Su 10, 3
58	Learn your facts!	To derive quickly or continue to derive quickly decimals that total 1 or 10.	Su 11, 2
59	Sum choice	To extend written methods to: subtraction of two integers less than 10 000.	Su 11, 4
60	Factors	To find all the pairs of factors of any number up to 100.	Su 12, 2

Collins Primary Maths © HarperCollins*Publishers* Ltd 2000

- Multiply and divide any positive integer up to 10 000 by 10 or 100 and understand the effect   HCM 1

Name _____   Date _____

Snake sum game

Fun with sums for one or two players.

How to play:
- Each player chooses a single-digit starting number.
- Write this number on your piece of paper.
- Take it in turns to roll the die and move your counter.
- Carry out the operation you have landed on using your starting number.
- The answer is your new number.
- If you cannot do the operation, then your number does not change.
- The winner is the player with the highest number at the end.

You will need:
- Paper, pencil and counter for each player.
- One 1–6 dice.

● Know by heart multiplication facts up to 10 × 10   HCM 2

Name _____   Date _____

Revising multiplication facts

Refresher

Multiply each number on the left by the number shown.
Match each number on the left to the correct product.

a ×3

3 •	• 9
7 •	• 27
9 •	• 12
1 •	• 18
6 •	• 3
8 •	• 21
4 •	• 6
2 •	• 15
5 •	• 24

b ×9

1 •	• 18
9 •	• 45
8 •	• 63
2 •	• 27
7 •	• 81
5 •	• 54
3 •	• 9
6 •	• 72
4 •	• 36

c ×4

1 •	• 12
3 •	• 32
6 •	• 20
8 •	• 4
5 •	• 28
9 •	• 16
7 •	• 36
4 •	• 24
2 •	• 8

Practice

Complete these number targets.

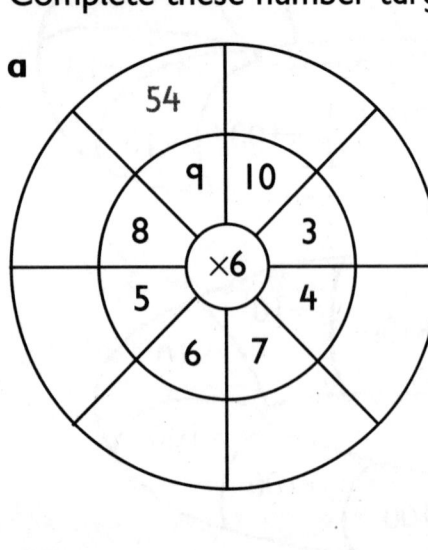

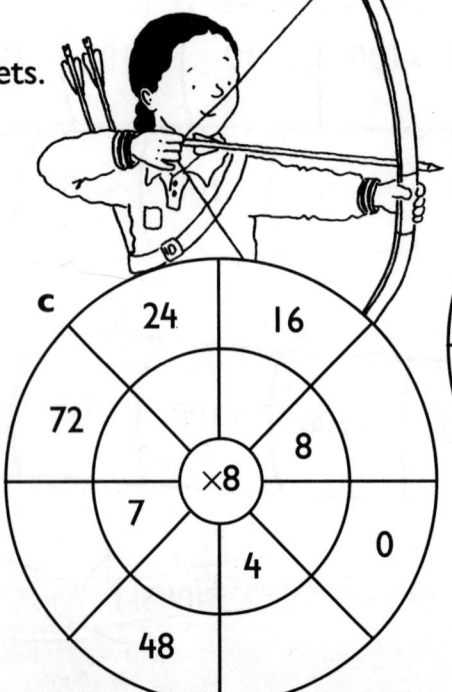

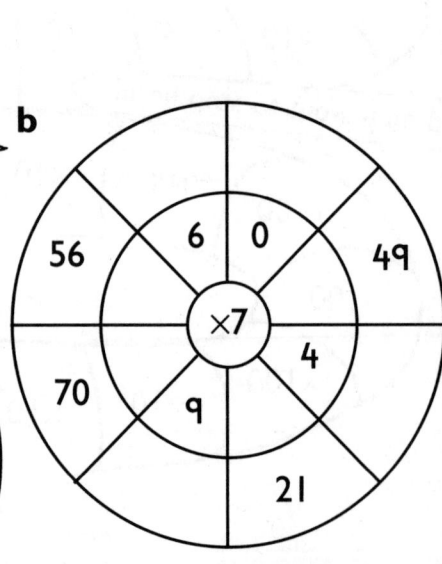

a — ×6 target: 54, 9, 10, 3, 4, 7, 6, 5, 8

b — ×7 target: 56, 6, 0, 49, 4, 9, 21, 70

c — ×8 target: 24, 16, 8, 0, 4, 48, 7, 72

● Derive quickly ... corresponding to tables up to 10 × 10   HCM 3

Name _____   Date _____

Revising multiplication and division

Refresher

Write the product for each set of numbers.

a 3 × 6 = 18
b 7 × 2
c 4 × 5
d 9 × 3
e 8 × 10

f 7 × 4
g 4 × 9
h 7 × 5
i 4 × 3
j 5 × 5

k 10 × 10
l 4 × 4
m 8 × 2
n 3 × 7
o 8 × 4

Practice

Fill in the missing operation: × or ÷

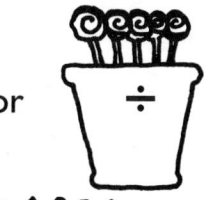

3 __ 3 = 9
27 __ 3 = 9
53 __ 5 = 10r3
36 __ 3 = 12
9 __ 4 = 36

8 __ 3 = 24
8 __ 2 = 4
12 __ 4 = 3
32 __ 4 = 8
20 __ 3 = 6r2

7 __ 4 = 28
5 __ 5 = 1
10 __ 10 = 100
47 __ 5 = 9r2
26 __ 4 = 6r2

12 __ 2 = 24
18 __ 3 = 6
24 __ 6 = 4
7 __ 3 = 21
14 __ 2 = 28

Collins Primary Maths © HarperCollinsPublishers Ltd 2000

HCM 4

- Use doubling or halving, starting from known facts

Name _____ Date _____

Doubling and halving

Refresher

Double or halve each number going into the machine to get a new number.

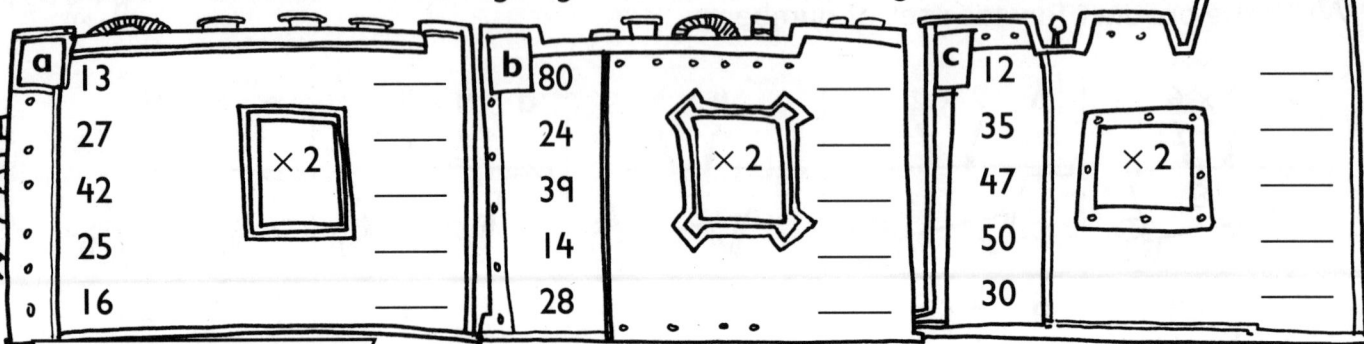

a
- 13
- 27
- 42
- 25
- 16

× 2

b
- 80
- 24
- 39
- 14
- 28

× 2

c
- 12
- 35
- 47
- 50
- 30

× 2

Practice

Start ⟶

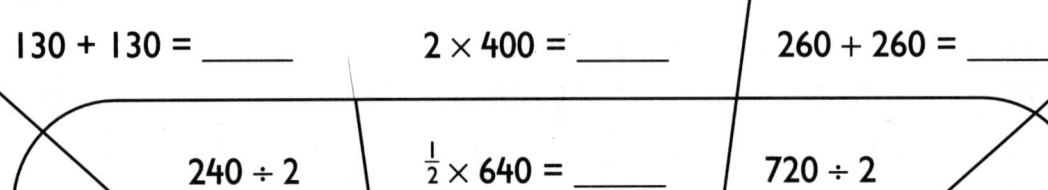

FIND YOUR WAY AROUND THE RACE TRACK

Answer the doubles on the outside track first.

Then halve the multiples of 10 and 100 on the inside track.

Outside track (starting from Start, going around):
- 130 + 130 = ____
- 2 × 400 = ____
- 260 + 260 = ____
- 80 + 80 = ____
- 2 × 500 = ____
- 120 × 2 = ____
- 180 + 180 = ____
- 430 + 430 = ____
- 2 × 250 = ____
- 390 + 390 = ____
- 400 × 2 = ____
- 110 × 2 = ____
- 600 × 2 = ____
- 470 × 2 = ____
- Finish

Inside track:
- 240 ÷ 2 = ____
- ½ × 640 = ____
- 720 ÷ 2 = ____
- ½ × 500 = ____
- ½ × 80 = ____
- 120 ÷ 2 = ____
- 860 ÷ 2 = ____
- 920 ÷ 2 = ____
- 700 ÷ 2 = ____
- ½ × 760 = ____
- ½ × 520 = ____
- 380 ÷ 2 = ____
- 420 − 210 = ____
- ½ × 340 = ____

Collins Primary Maths © HarperCollinsPublishers Ltd 2000

HCM 5

Name _____ **Date** _____

Helpful doubles

Refresher

Complete each number fact for 8 by multiplying by 4, then doubling your answer.

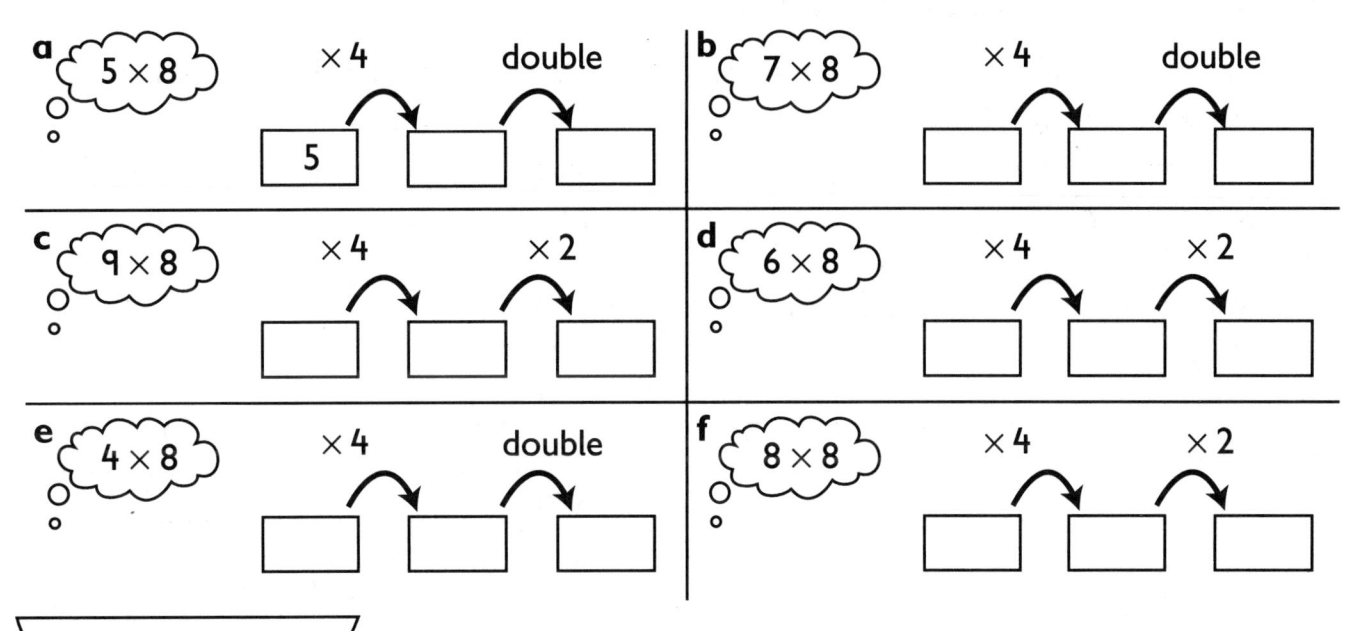

a 5×8 — ×4 → [5] — double → [ ] [ ]

b 7×8 — ×4 → [ ] — double → [ ]

c 9×8 — ×4 → [ ] — ×2 → [ ]

d 6×8 — ×4 → [ ] — ×2 → [ ]

e 4×8 — ×4 → [ ] — double → [ ]

f 8×8 — ×4 → [ ] — ×2 → [ ]

Practice

Complete each number fact for 16 by multiplying by 8, then doubling your answer.

a 5×16 — ×8 → [5] — double → [ ] [ ]

b 3×16 — ×8 → [ ] — double → [ ]

c 10×16 — ×8 → [ ] — ×2 → [ ]

d 4×16 — ×8 → [ ] — ×2 → [ ]

e 6×16 — ×8 → [ ] — double → [ ]

f 8×16 — ×8 → [ ] — ×2 → [ ]

g 7×16 — ×8 → [ ] — ×2 → [ ]

h 9×16 — ×8 → [ ] — double → [ ]

• Use doubling or halving, starting from known facts

Collins Primary Maths © HarperCollinsPublishers Ltd 2000

• Recognise when two simple fractions are equivalent

HCM 6

Name _____ Date _____

Wall fractions

Refresher

These walls have been built with each row of bricks divided into different fractions.

1. On this wall find the rows where you can shade a **half**. Label the fractions you shade. Put a cross in the box if you can't shade in a half.

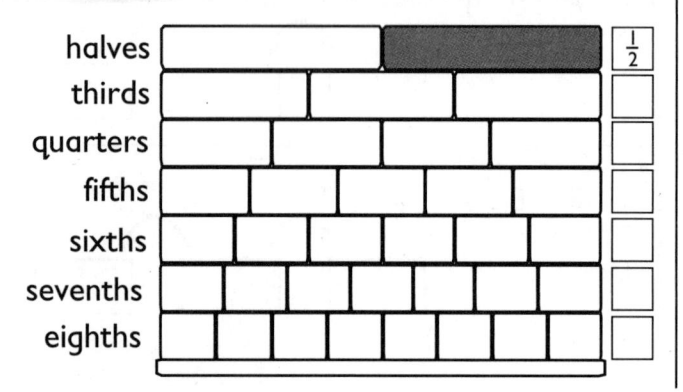

2. On this wall find the rows where you can shade a **quarter**. Label the fractions you shade. Put a cross in the box if you can't shade in a quarter.

halves — $\frac{1}{2}$
thirds
quarters
fifths
sixths
sevenths
eighths

halves
thirds
quarters — $\frac{1}{4}$
fifths
sixths
sevenths
eighths

Practice

1. On this wall find the rows where you can shade a **third**. Label the fractions you shade. Put a cross in the box if you can't shade in a third.

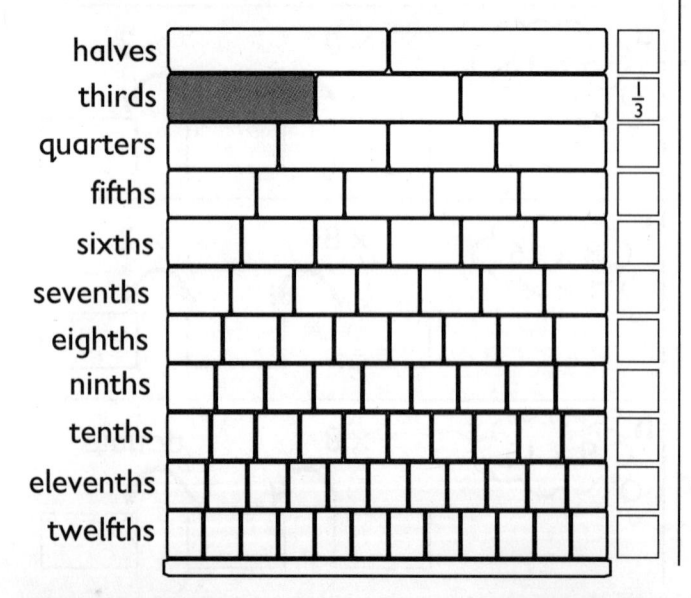

2. On this wall find the rows where you can shade a **fifth**. Label the fractions you shade. Put a cross in the box if you can't shade in a fifth.

halves
thirds — $\frac{1}{3}$
quarters
fifths
sixths
sevenths
eighths
ninths
tenths
elevenths
twelfths

halves
thirds
quarters
fifths — $\frac{1}{5}$
sixths
sevenths
eighths
ninths
tenths
elevenths
twelfths

Collins Primary Maths © HarperCollinsPublishers Ltd 2000

● Know what each digit represents in a number with up to two decimal places   HCM 7

Name _____   Date _____

Decimals in order

Refresher

1 Use these digits to make six decimal numbers.

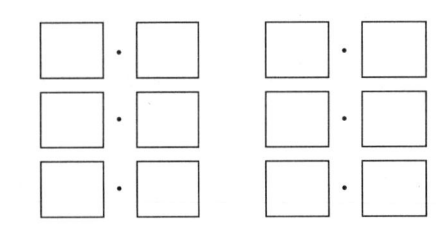

   3   7   5

2 Put your numbers in order from smallest to largest.

Practice

1 Use these digits to make six decimal numbers.

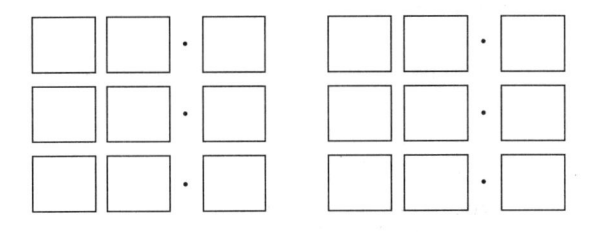

   4   9   1   8

2 Put your numbers in order from smallest to largest.
   Write down a number that comes between.

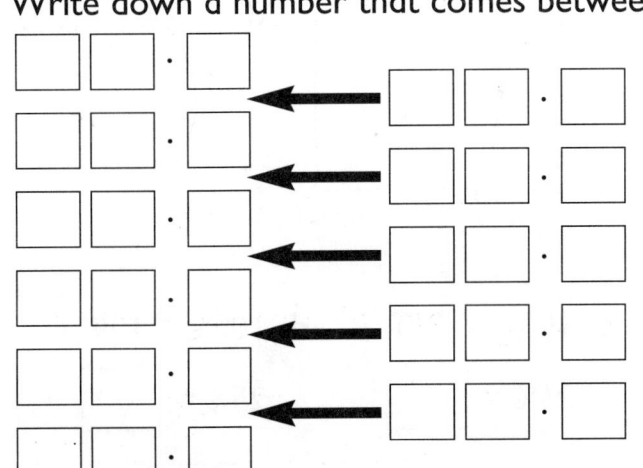

● Begin to understand percentage as the number of parts in every 100   HCM 8

Name _____   Date _____

Percentages

Look around your home. Can you find any percentages?
Look in the food cupboard on boxes, packets and tins.
Look in newspapers and magazines. Write any you find.

Refresher

1 Shade in 50% of these shapes.

   a   b    c 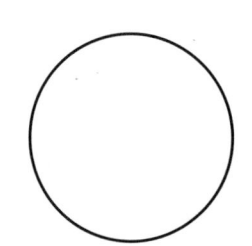   d

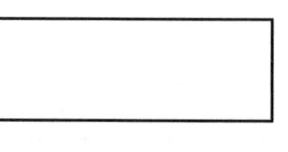

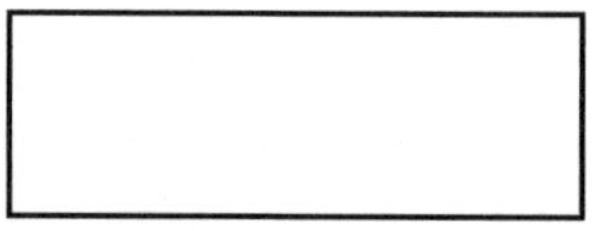

2 Find 50% of these amounts.

   a 100% = 6   b 100% = 26   c 100% = 60   d 100% = 32
      50% = ☐   50% = ☐   50% = ☐   50% = ☐

Practice

1 Shade in 25% of these shapes.

   a   b 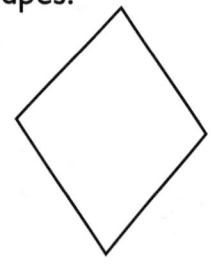   c   d

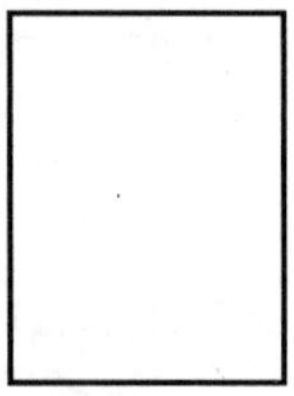

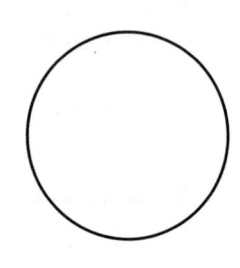

2 Find 25% of these amounts.

   a 100% = 84   b 100% = 48   c 100% = 200   d 100% = 104
      25% = ☐   25% = ☐   25% = ☐   25% = ☐

Collins Primary Maths © HarperCollinsPublishers Ltd 2000

● Solve simple problems involving ratio and proportion HCM 9

Name _____ Date _____

Ratio problems

Refresher

1. Tom's dad has bought 24 sweets. As Tom is older than his sister Julie, his dad gives him 3 sweets for every 1 he gives Julie.
Complete the table to work out how many sweets they're both given.

Julie	Tom
1	3

2. For every bone Nellie has, she eats 1 and buries 6. She has had 35 bones so far. How many has she buried and how many has she eaten?
Complete the table to help you work out the problem.

eaten	buried
1	6

Practice

1. Out of every 5 stickers I buy, I keep 2 and swap 3. I have bought 50 in the last few weeks. How many have I kept? ☐
How many have I swapped? ☐
Complete the table to help you work out the problem.

How many would I have kept if I had bought 75? How many would I have swapped?

keep	swap
2	3

2. Apples come in bags of 8. I eat 6 out of every bag and give 2 to my rabbit. If I buy 6 bags, how many apples do I eat altogether? ☐
How many does my rabbit eat altogether? ☐

me	rabbit
6	2

Collins Primary Maths © HarperCollinsPublishers Ltd 2000

● Solve a problem by representing and interpreting data in tables, charts, graphs and diagrams   HCM 10

Name _____   Date _____

Bat bar line charts

Refresher

Bat nests are called roosts. The bar line chart shows the bats in roosts in 1999. Copy and complete the table.

Bats	Roosts
0	
1	
2	
3	
4	
5	
6	

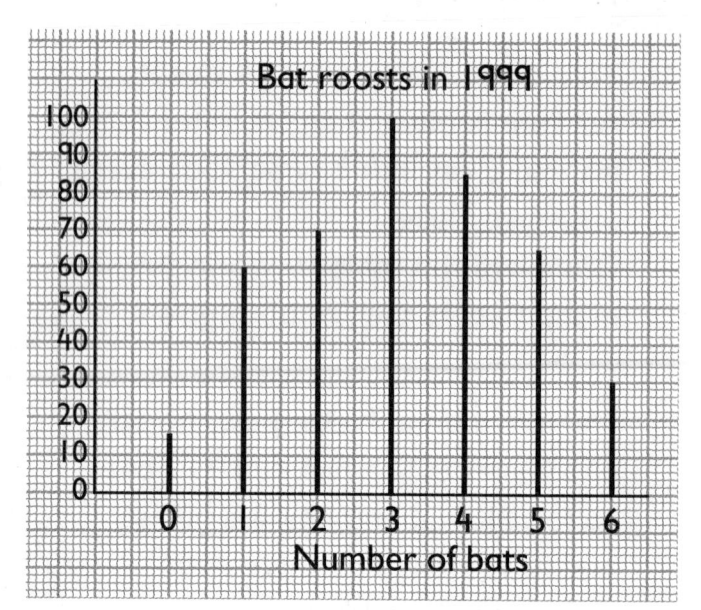

Bat roosts in 1999

Practice

1 The table shows the bats in roosts in 2000. Copy and complete the bar line chart.

Bats	Roosts
0	5
1	16
2	72
3	54
4	43
5	29
6	11

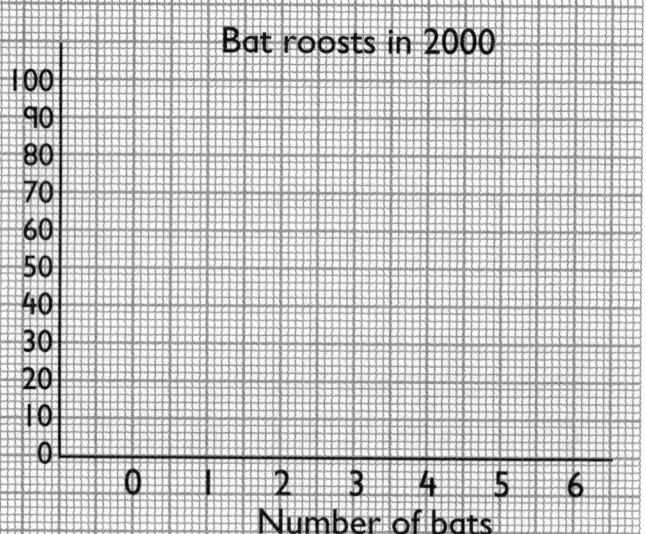

Bat roosts in 2000

2 Now answer these questions.

   a How many roosts had 4 bats in 1999?

   b How many roosts were empty in 2000?

   c How many roosts had less than 3 bats in 1999?

   d What was the most common (mode) roost size in 2000?

   e What is the mode for 1999?

   f How many bats were there altogether in 1999?

   g Were there more or less bats in 2000?

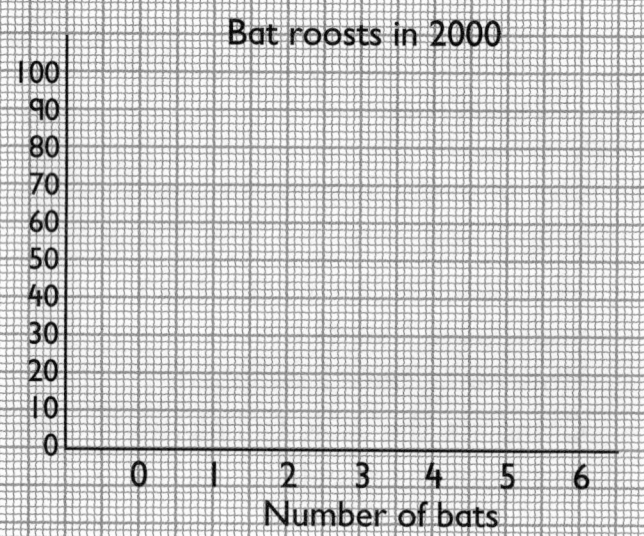

● Develop calculator skills and use a calculator effectively   HCM 11

Name _____ Date _____

Calculating clothes costs

Refresher

Use your calculator to work out these.

1 a £3·28 + £2·56 = ☐   b £1·85 + £2.14 = ☐   c £9·99 + £7·24 = ☐
2 a £9·31 − £4·85 = ☐   b £3·09 − £1.36 = ☐   c £5·87 − £3·99 = ☐
3 a 3 × £1·85 = ☐   b 2 × £65·16 = ☐   c 9 × £3·39 = ☐

Practice

Skirt £12·72   Tie £3·88   Coat £23·99   Gloves £4·80   Scarf £5·72

1 Calculate the cost of:
   a A tie and coat _____   b A skirt and gloves _____   c A scarf and tie _____
   d Four ties _____   e Two coats _____   f Gloves, a coat and a skirt _____

2 Calculate the difference in price between:
   a A skirt and a coat _____
   b Gloves and a tie _____
   c A skirt and a scarf _____

3 Find the change from a £10 note when you buy:
   a A tie _____   b A scarf _____   c Gloves _____

4 Find the total cost for this clothes bill:

Trousers	£14·23
Dress	£16·30
Shirt	£8·00
Tie	£4·05
Jumper	£9·99
Total:	

5 Calculate the cost of one pair of socks:

   3 pairs of socks £2·94

• Solve mathematical problems or puzzles ... HCM 12

Name _____ Date _____

Flexing rectangles

Refresher and Practice

You need:
- scissors, sticky tape

1. Cut out the large rectangle at the foot of the page.
2. Copy these numbers and letters.

...on the front

1	1	2	3
3	2	1	1
1	1	2	3

...on the back

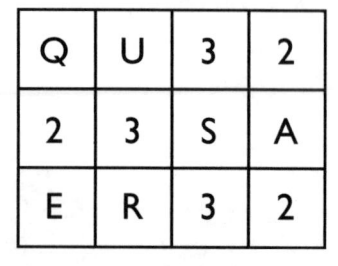

Q	U	3	2
2	3	S	A
E	R	3	2

3. Cut along the dark lines.

1	1	2	3
3	2	1	1
1	1	2	3

4. Fold the middle section back.

1	1	2	3
3	3		1
1	1	2	3

5. Fold the right-hand column back. Then fold it back again.

1	1	2	
3	3		2
1	1	2	

6. Fold the left-hand square in. Carefully join the two middle squares with tape.

1	1
3	3	1
1	1

1	1
1	1
1	1

7. You can see all the 1s. Find the face with all the 2s. Now "flex" the shape to find the face with all the 3s then the face with all the letters. Unscramble the letters to find the name of a mathematical shape.

● Classify triangles (isosceles, equilateral, scalene), using criteria such as equal sides, equal angles   HCM 13

Name _____   Date _____

Folding triangles

Refresher and Practice

1 Cut out the triangles at the bottom of the page.
   Write the name of each triangle inside the shape.

2 **Investigate by folding only**, and write which triangle has:

   a 3 sides equal in length   _____

   b 2 equal sides   _____

   c no 2 sides equal   _____

   d 1 line of symmetry   _____

   e 3 lines of symmetry   _____

   f no lines of symmetry   _____

   g all angles equal in size   _____

   h all angles different in size _____

   i 2 equal angles   _____

Practice

Complete this table.

Triangle	Number of equal sides	Number of equal angles	Number of lines of symmetry
isoceles			
equilateral			
scalene			

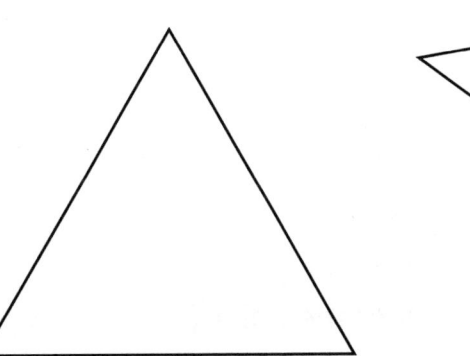

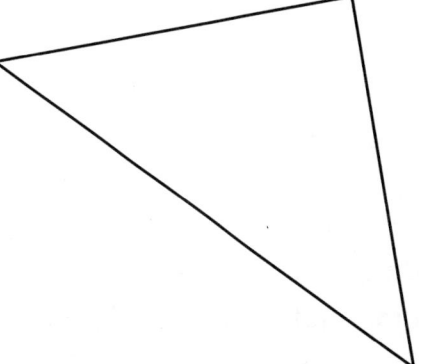

Collins Primary Maths © HarperCollinsPublishers Ltd 2000

● Read and plot co-ordinates in the first quadrant

HCM 14

Name _____ Date _____

Plotting shapes

Refresher and Practice

1 For each grid, plot the points and join them in order with straight lines.

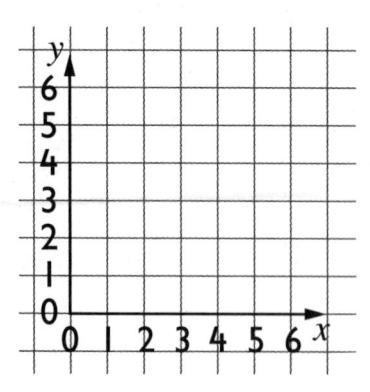

a (1, 4) (3, 6) (6, 2) (1, 4)
Name of shape_____

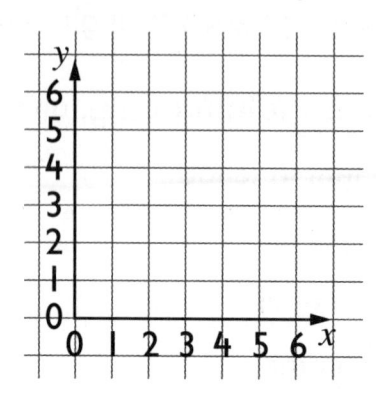

b (2, 2) (2, 5) (6, 6) (6, 2) (2, 2)
Name of shape_____

Practice

1 Three of the vertices of a rectangle are plotted on each grid. Find the 4th vertex.

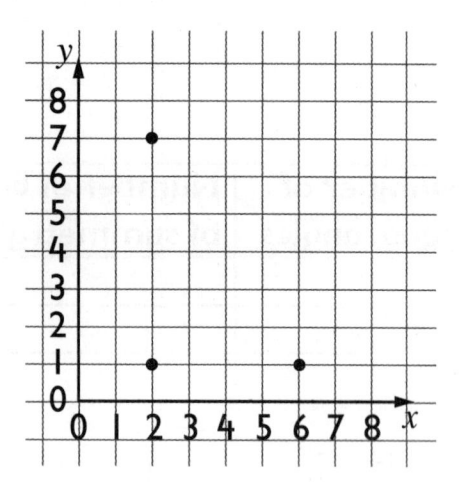

a The co-ordinates are:
_____

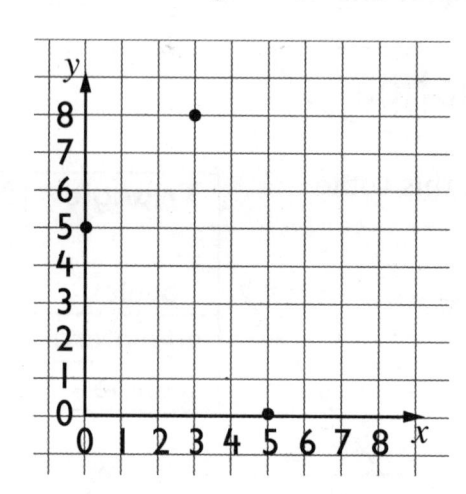

b The co-ordinates are:
_____

2 For each rectangle, draw the diagonals.
The diagonals of rectangle a cross at the point (,)
The diagonals of rectangle b cross at the point (,)

Collins Primary Maths © HarperCollinsPublishers Ltd 2000

● Understand, measure and calculate perimeters of rectangles and regular polygons   HCM 15

Name _____   Date _____

Chessboard perimeters

Refresher and Practice

This chessboard is square. Each side measures 40 cm.

1   Find and record these measurements.
    a   length of side of chessboard   _____ cm.
    b   perimeter of chessboard   _____ cm.
    c   length of side of one small square   _____ cm.
    d   perimeter of one small square   _____ cm.

Practice

These squares grow from the bottom left-hand corner of the chessboard.

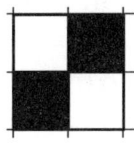

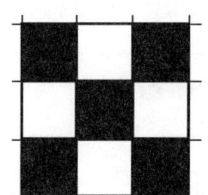

2   Continue this pattern further.

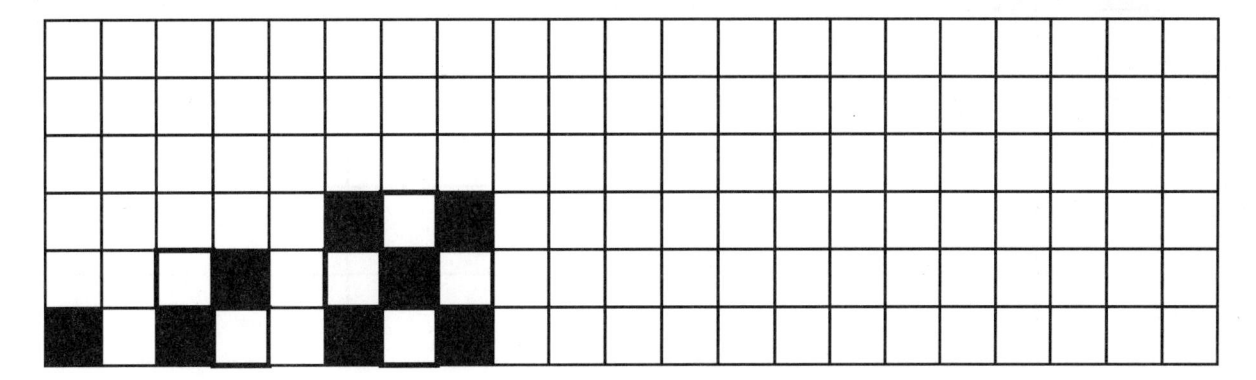

3   Complete this table.

Number of squares	1	2	3	4	5	6	7	8
Length of side in cm	5							
Perimeter in cm	20							

4   Look at your last answer in the table and your answer to question 1b. Explain why this is.

_____

Collins Primary Maths © HarperCollinsPublishers Ltd 2000

HCM 16

Name _____ Date _____

Measuring money

Refresher and Practice

You can measure the diameter of a coin to the nearest millimetre like this.

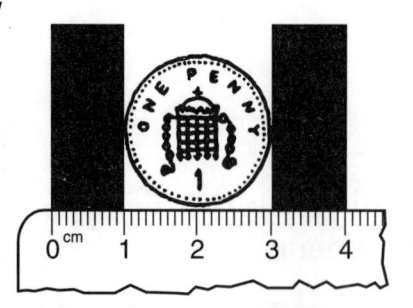

Measure the diameter of these coins to the nearest millimetre.
Record your measurements in 3 ways each time.

value of coin	☐ mm	☐ cm ☐ mm	☐ . ☐ cm
1p			
2p			
5p			
10p			
£1			

Practice

1. A school is raising money by collecting 1 kilometre of 1p coins.
   The coins are placed to form straight lines.
   How much money do they raise with:

   a 1 metre of 1p coins? _____   b 10 metres of 1p coins? _____

   c 100 metres of 1p coins? _____ d 1 kilometre of 1p coins? _____

● Read the time on a 24-hour digital clock and use 24-hour clock notation such as 19:53   HCM 17

Name _____   Date _____

TV times

Refresher and Practice

1. Convert these 24-hour digital clock times to 12-hour clock times, adding a.m. or p.m.

24-hour clock	07:15	15:33	10:42	22:10	12:50
12-hour clock	7:15 a.m.	_____	_____	_____	_____

2. Convert the 12-hour clock times to 24-hour digital clock times.

12-hour clock	9:35a.m.	11:27a.m.	16:40p.m.	5:55a.m.	11:06p.m.
24-hour clock	_____	_____	_____	_____	_____

Practice

1. You have a 3-hour video tape.
   Look up this evening's TV guide. Choose 5 programmes you wish to video. Write the channel and the start and finish times you will enter into the video recorder.

Programme	Channel	Start time	Finish time	Duration
Example: Neighbours	1	17:35	18:00	25 min
1				
2				
3				
4				
5				

2. Calculate the length of each programme and record in the "duration" column.

3. Work out how many minutes are still left in your video tape.
   Answer: _____ mins.

• Use informal pencil and paper methods to support, record or explain additions

HCM 18

Name _____ Date _____

Adding up in the air

Refresher

Write these calulations out vertically and then work out the answer. The first two have been written out for you.

a 462 + 253 = ☐
    462
  + 253
  ―――

b 285 + 164 = ☐
    285
  + 164
  ―――

c 327 + 245 = ☐

d 352 + 366 = ☐

e 568 + 128 = ☐

f 318 + 273 = ☐

g 295 + 364 = ☐

h 429 + 269 = ☐

i 487 + 265 = ☐

Practice

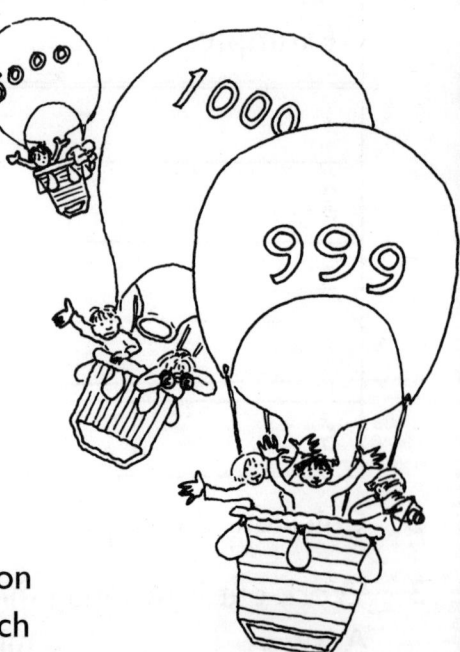

1 Write five three-digit numbers between 100 and 999.

  ☐ ☐ ☐ ☐ ☐

2 Write five four-digit numbers between 1000 and 5000.

  ☐ ☐ ☐ ☐ ☐

3 Use these numbers to make up and work out six addition calculations. Choose one number from each box for each calculation. Write the calculations on the back of the sheet.

Collins Primary Maths © HarperCollinsPublishers Ltd 2000

● ● Use all four operations to solve simple word problems ...   HCM 19

Name _____   Date _____

In the playground

Refresher

1. 84 children have brought skipping ropes to school today and 37 have brought balls.
   How many toys altogether in the playground? ☐

2. There are 274 infants and 359 juniors in the playground.
   How many children altogether? ☐

3. There are 276 girls at school today. 138 of them are in the hall eating their dinner.
   How many are out in the playground? ☐

4. There are 138 girls eating their dinner and 247 children altogether in the dinner hall.
   How many boys are there? ☐

Working

Practice

1. 377 children came out to play.
   The infants go in early as they are going on a trip.
   There are 186 children left in the playground.
   How many infants came out to play? ☐

2. 451 children brought their coats to school today.
   183 infants are wearing their coats and 204 juniors are wearing theirs.
   How many coats are left in the cloakrooms? ☐

3. There are 409 children out in the playground. 56 are playing football, 178 are running around playing chase and 103 are skipping.
   How many are doing something else? ☐

4. 165 infants and 211 juniors want to play on the grass. Only 285 children are allowed on the grass at one time.
   How many children will be disappointed? ☐

Working

Collins Primary Maths © HarperCollinsPublishers Ltd 2000

● Recognise and extend number sequences   HCM 20

Name _____   Date _____

Number sequences

Refresher

Fill in the missing numbers in each sequence.
Write the rule in the box.

a 12, 23, 34, ___, ___, ___, ___, ___, ___, ___.   +11

b 91, ___, ___, 97, ___, ___, 103, 105, ___, ___.   ☐

c 16, 6, ___, ___, ___, ___, ___, ___, ___, ___.   ☐

d 25, 16, 7, ___, ___, ___, ___, ___, ___, ___.   ☐

e 72, 66, 60, ___, ___, ___, ___, ___, ___, ___.   ☐

f 30, 34, 38, ___, ___, ___, ___, ___, ___, ___.   ☐

g −15, −11, ___, −3, ___, ___, ___, ___, ___, ___.   ☐

h −96, ___, ___, ___, ___, ___, ___, −26, ___, −6.   ☐

Practice

Fill in the missing numbers by following the rules given.

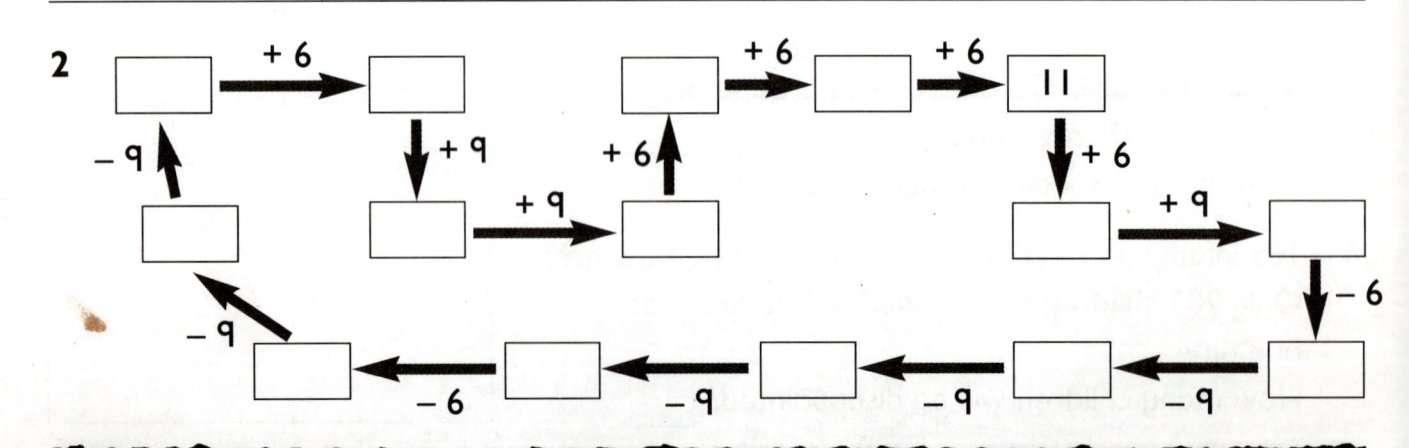

1. Starting at 0, following arrows with +6, +9, +6, +9, +6, −9, −6, −9, −9, +6 around the loop.

2. Loop with rules +6, +6, +6, +6, +6, −9, +9, +6, +9, −6, −9, −9, −9, −6, −9 and the value 11 shown in one box.

Collins Primary Maths © HarperCollinsPublishers Ltd 2000

● Know squares of numbers to at least 10 × 10   HCM 21

Name _____ Date _____

Square numbers

Refresher

Complete the flowers by filling in the missing square number factor or product.

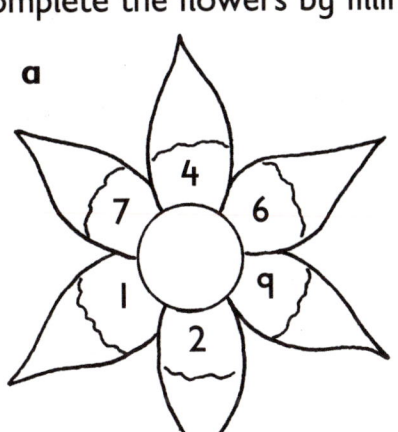

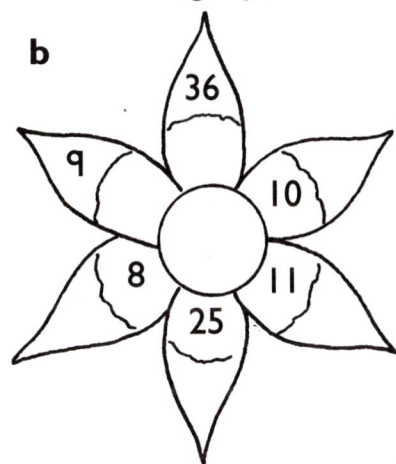

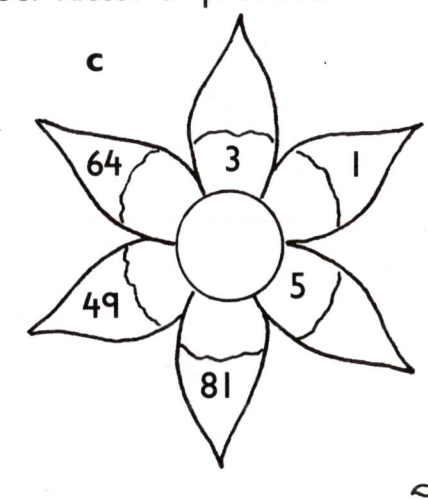

a (flower with petals: 4, 7, 6, 1, 9, 2)

b (flower with petals: 36, 9, 10, 8, 11, 25)

c (flower with petals: 64, 3, 1, 49, 5, 81)

Practice

1 Answer these questions. Write a multiplication fact and answer.

  a What is 7 squared? _____

  b Which number multiplied by itself gives 64? _____

  c What is 1^2? _____

  d What is the square of 4? _____

  e What is larger, 8^2 or 49? _____

  f What is the area of a square with one side 9 cm long? _____

  g What is the square of 6? _____

2 Use your knowledge of square numbers to work out the answers to these questions.

  a $4^2 + 36 =$ ☐   f $5^2 + 5^2 =$ ☐

  b $7^2 + 7^2 =$ ☐   g ☐ $- 3^2 = 91$

  c $2^2 + 8^2 =$ ☐   h ☐ $- 4^2 = 36$

  d $10^2 - 49 =$ ☐   i ☐ $+ 7^2 = 100$

  e $9^2 - 18 =$ ☐   j ☐ $+ 7^2 = 97$

Working

Collins Primary Maths © HarperCollinsPublishers Ltd 2000

Spot the pairs

Refresher

Find 5 pairs of numbers that have been multiplied or divided by 10. Write them as 5 division calculations and 5 multiplication calculations.

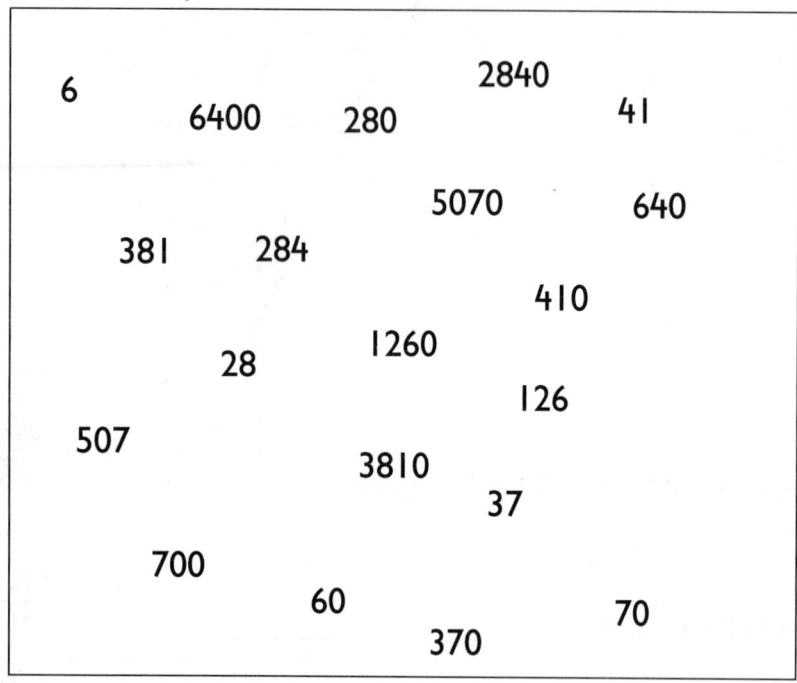

```
    6              2840
         6400  280       41
                  5070      640
      381   284
                      410
              1260
         28           126
   507
              3810
                   37
         700
              60            70
                   370
```

1 Example: 41 × 10 = 410
2 ____
3 ____
4 ____
5 ____
6 ____
7 ____
8 ____
9 ____
10 ____

Practice

Find 5 pairs of numbers that have been multiplied or divided by 100. Write them as 5 division calculations and 5 multiplication calculations.

```
              800
      86              28      15
            219
  83400              512         6133
         126800
  2800                    8600
            51200
       613300        834
  80000      21900     1500    1268
```

1 Example: 80 000 ÷ 100 = 800
2 ____
3 ____
4 ____
5 ____
6 ____
7 ____
8 ____
9 ____
10 ____

● Derive quickly ... division facts corresponding to tables up to 10 × 10   HCM 23

Name _____   Date _____

Facts reminder

Refresher

1 a Fill in the missing number in each triangle so that each number relates to the other.
   b Write a multiplication and division fact for each.

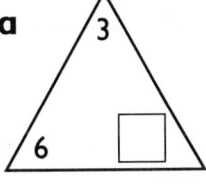

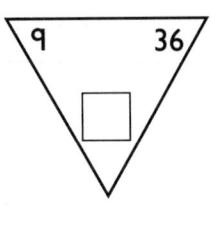

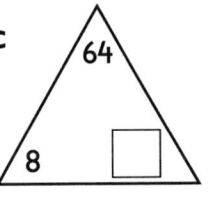

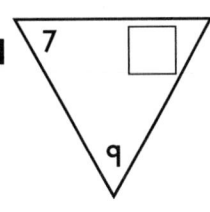

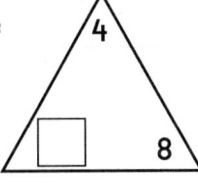

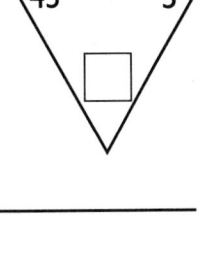

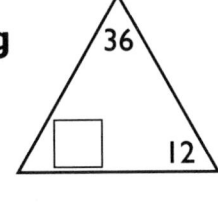

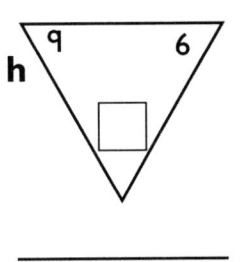

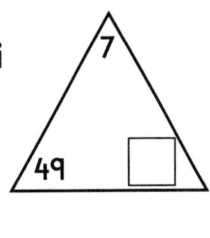

a [triangle: 3, 6, □]
$3 \times 6 = \square$
$\square \div 3 = 6$

b [triangle: 9, 36, □]

c [triangle: 64, 8, □]

d [triangle: 7, □, 9]

e [triangle: 4, □, 8]

f [triangle: 45, 5, □]

g [triangle: 36, □, 12]

h [triangle: 9, 6, □]

i [triangle: 7, 49, □]

j [triangle: 48, □, 8]

Practice

1 Write down the calculation, then work out the answer.

a 7 multiplied by 6

b the product of 5 and 9

c 3 times more than 4

d share 27 between 3

e 34 divided by 4 gives remainder of

f what divided by 7 equals 4

g the quotient of 36 and 6

h the product of 8 and 3

i the factors of 21

j the quotient of 60 and 5

Collins Primary Maths © HarperCollinsPublishers Ltd 2000

● Use closely related facts (e.g. multiply by 19 or 21 by multiplying by 20 and adjusting)   HCM 24

Name _____ Date _____

Terrific 20s treasure hunt

Refresher

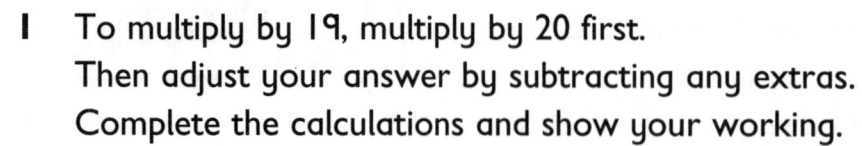

$7 \times 19 = (7 \times 20) - 7$
$= 140 - 7$
$= 133$

1. To multiply by 19, multiply by 20 first.
   Then adjust your answer by subtracting any extras.
   Complete the calculations and show your working.

   a) $18 \times 19 = $ _____
   b) $24 \times 19 = $ _____
   c) $35 \times 19 = $ _____

$8 \times 21 = (8 \times 20) + 8$
$= 160 + 8$
$= 168$

2. To multiply by 21, multiply by 20 first.
   Then adjust your answer by adding any extras.
   Complete the calculations and show your working.

   a) $15 \times 21 = $ _____
   b) $27 \times 21 = $ _____
   c) $44 \times 21 = $ _____

Practice

Find your way round the treasure hunt by multiplying by 20 first and then adjusting. Try to work out the answers in your head.

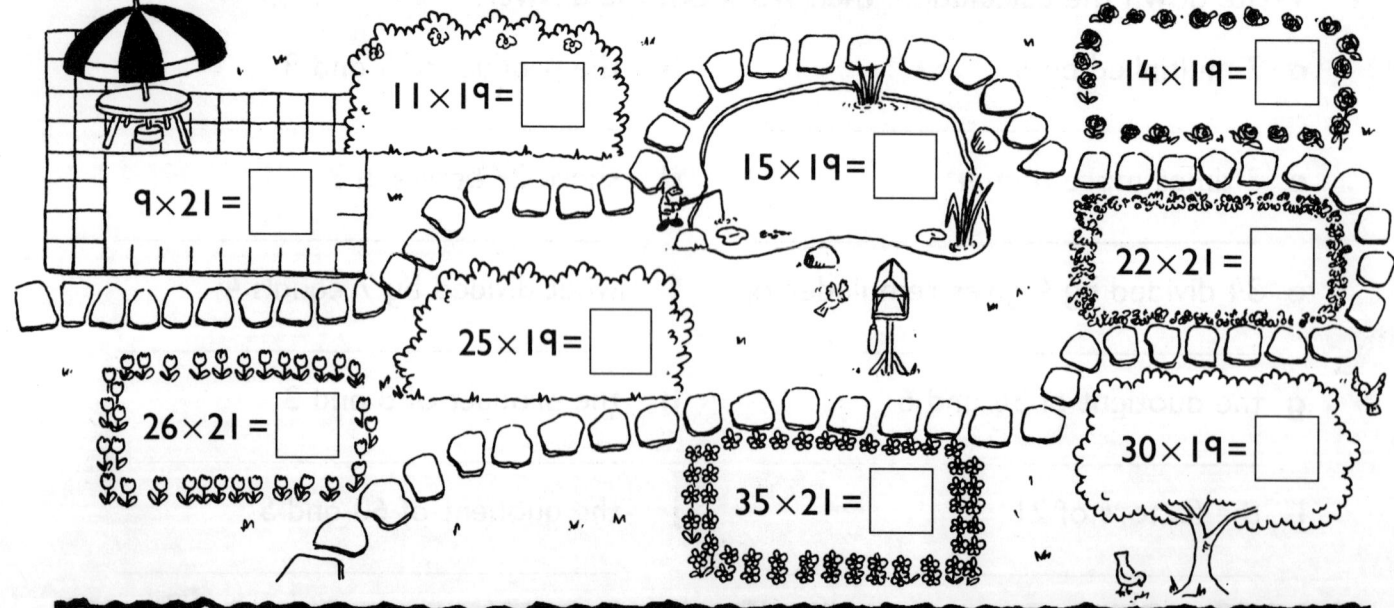

$11 \times 19 = $ ☐
$9 \times 21 = $ ☐
$15 \times 19 = $ ☐
$14 \times 19 = $ ☐
$25 \times 19 = $ ☐
$22 \times 21 = $ ☐
$26 \times 21 = $ ☐
$35 \times 21 = $ ☐
$30 \times 19 = $ ☐

Collins Primary Maths © HarperCollinsPublishers Ltd 2000

● Extend written methods to short division of HTU by U   HCM 25

Name _____   Date _____

Recording division

Refresher

1 Approximate the answer to each calculation.
   Show the calculation you used.

a 268 ÷ 4

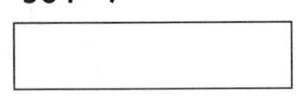

b 519 ÷ 9

c 221 ÷ 3

d 384 ÷ 8

e 457 ÷ 5

f 287 ÷ 6

g 676 ÷ 7

h 299 ÷ 8

i 364 ÷ 7

j 785 ÷ 9

Practice

For each calculation, write the approximate answer first,
then use the standard written method of division to record your work.

a 456 ÷ 7

7) 456

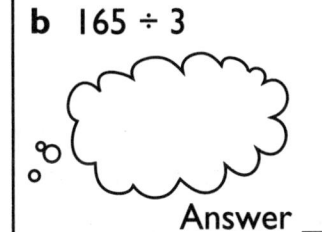

Answer _____

b 165 ÷ 3

3) 165

Answer _____

c 686 ÷ 8

8) 686

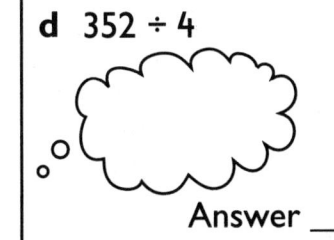

Answer _____

d 352 ÷ 4

4) 352

Answer _____

e 387 ÷ 9

9) 387

Answer _____

f 465 ÷ 5

5) 465

Answer _____

Collins Primary Maths © HarperCollinsPublishers Ltd 2000

● Make simple conversions of pounds to foreign currency [OK?]　　　　　　　　HCM 26

Name _____ Date _____

Holiday money

Refresher

1 Find the tourist rates in the business section of a recent newspaper.
   Cut it out and staple it to the corner of this page.

2 What currency is used in:
   a Greece _____
   b Australia _____
   c Spain _____
   d Italy _____
   e Portugal _____

3 What is the exchange rate for one:
   a US dollar _____
   b French franc _____
   c German mark _____
   d Japanese yen _____
   e Singapore dollar _____

Practice

1 Complete the tables below to show how much of each
   currency you receive when you exchange English pounds.
   Round each currency rate to the nearest whole number if you need to.

a

Australian Dollars £1 = $2·5	
£5	
£25	
£50	

b

French franks £1 = 9·67	
£5	
£25	
£50	

c

Mexican Pesos £1 = 14·6	
£5	
£10	
£100	

d

German Marks £1 = 3·2	
£5	
£25	
£50	

e

Belgian Francs £1 = 64·3	
£5	
£10	
£100	

Collins Primary Maths © HarperCollinsPublishers Ltd 2000

● Relate fractions to division, and use division to find simple fractions   HCM 27

Name _____   Date _____

Fraction pairs game

- Cut out the cards along the dotted lines.
- Shuffle the cards and place them face down on the table.
- Each player takes turns to choose two cards. If one of the numbers is a fraction of the other, keep the pair. If it is not, put both cards back in the same place.
- Keep playing until all the cards have been chosen. The winner is the player with the most pairs.

Refresher

Play with the top set of cards only. These involve halves, quarters and thirds.

Practice

Play with all the cards. These involve halves, quarters, thirds, tenths, hundredths and sixths.

22	11	600	200	60	15	4	1	14
7	70	35	200	50	100	300		
80	8	900	90	36	6	210		
21	430	43	7600	76	5800	58		

11 is half of 22

Collins Primary Maths © HarperCollinsPublishers Ltd 2000

● Order a set of numbers with the same number of decimal places   HCM 28

Name _____ Date _____

Decimal pathways

Find three paths through the numbers from start to finish.
You can move in any direction but the decimals must be in order.

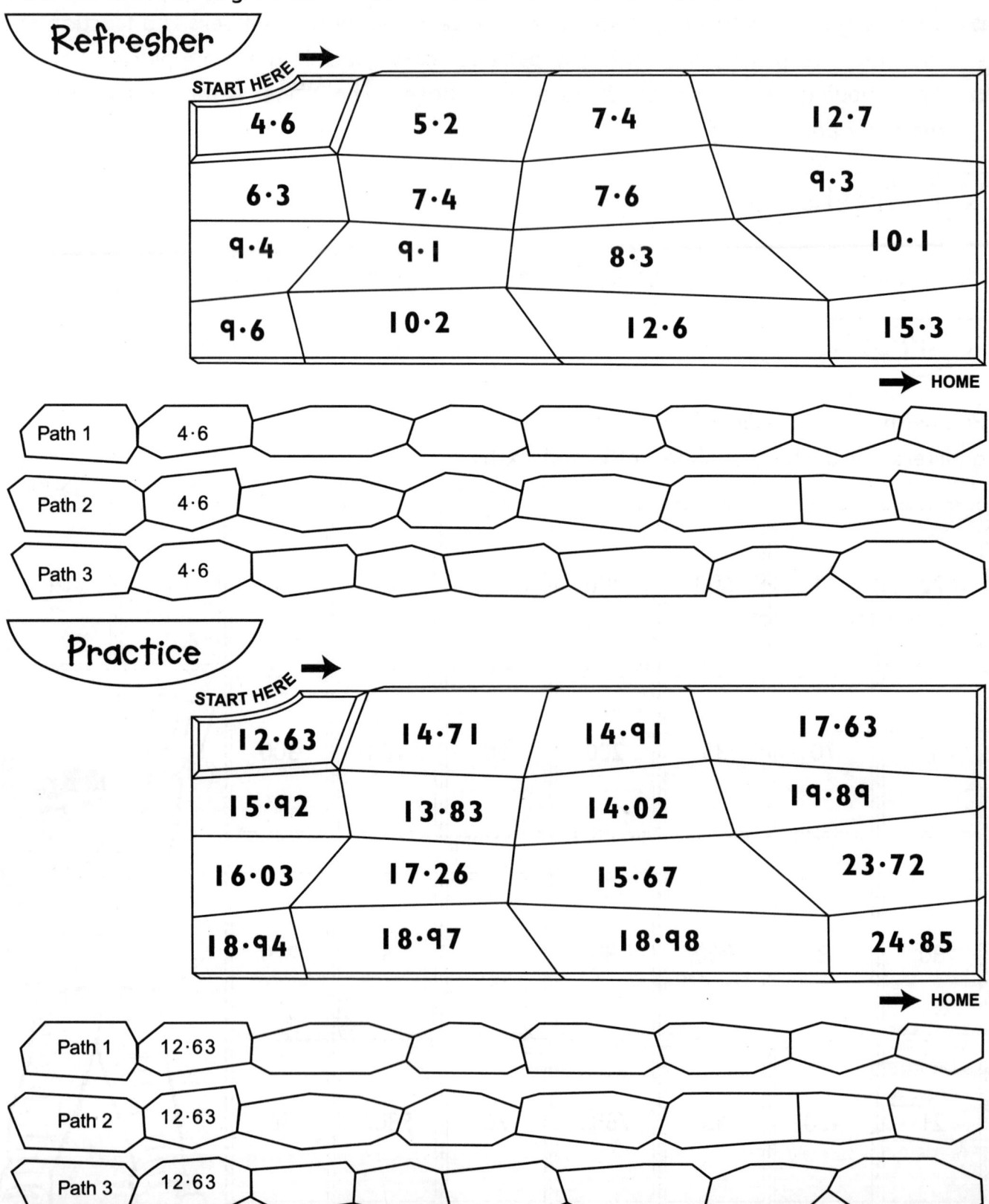

Refresher

START HERE →

4·6	5·2	7·4	12·7
6·3	7·4	7·6	9·3
9·4	9·1	8·3	10·1
9·6	10·2	12·6	15·3

→ HOME

Path 1 4·6
Path 2 4·6
Path 3 4·6

Practice

START HERE →

12·63	14·71	14·91	17·63
15·92	13·83	14·02	19·89
16·03	17·26	15·67	23·72
18·94	18·97	18·98	24·85

→ HOME

Path 1 12·63
Path 2 12·63
Path 3 12·63

Collins Primary Maths © HarperCollinsPublishers Ltd 2000

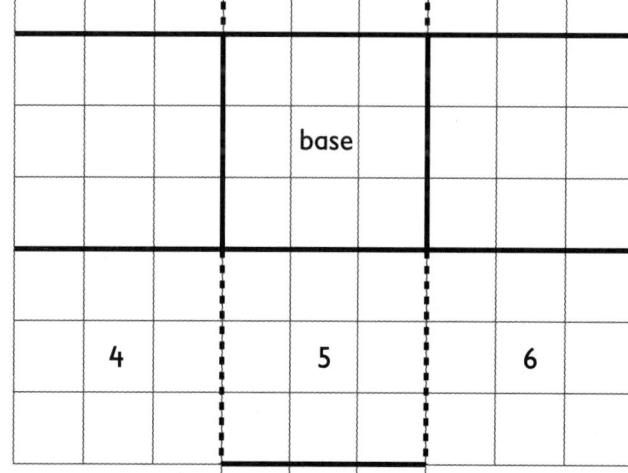

● Visualise 3D shapes from 2D drawings and identify nets for an open cube   HCM 29

Name _____ Date _____

Open cubes

Refresher and Practice

1 Large net.
   Carefully cut out the large net.
   Cut along the dotted lines.
   Score the bold black lines.

2 To make your open cube:
   ● fold 1 inside 2 inside 3
   ● fold 7 inside 1
   ● put 8 on the base
   ● fold 4 inside 5 inside 6
   ● fold 9 inside 4
   ● put 10 on the base

Practice

Repeat, as above for the small net.

Collins Primary Maths © HarperCollinsPublishers Ltd 2000

● Recognise directions

HCM 30

Name _____ Date _____

Dazzling diagonals

Refresher

Remember to use a ruler

1. For each hexagon, draw straight lines to join the vertex marked by the black dot to the three non-adjacent vertices.

2. Check each diagram for triangles with just two equal sides. Colour these triangles red.

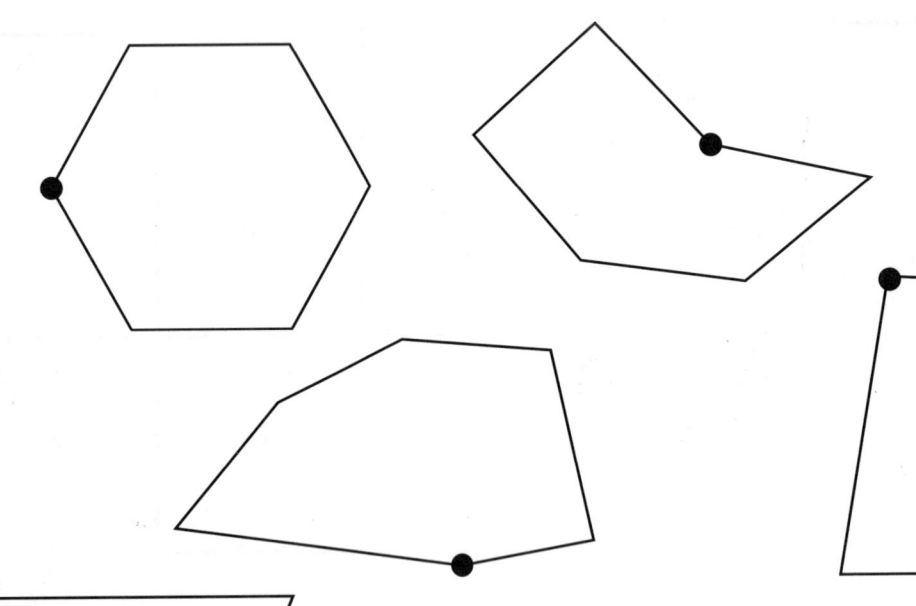

Practice

1. Use straight lines to join the points 1 to 2, 2 to 3, 3 to 4 and so on.

2. Count the number of sides the shape has. Answer: _____ sides

3. Draw all the diagonals, joining non-adjacent vertices with straight lines.

4. Count the number of diagonals at each vertex. Answer: _____ diagonals

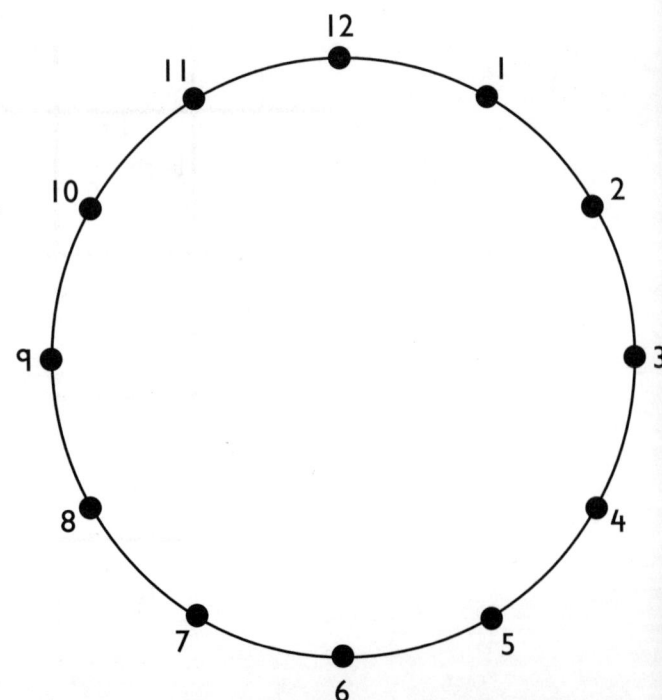

Collins Primary Maths © HarperCollinsPublishers Ltd 2000

Making patterns from rotating shapes

HCM 31

Name _____ Date _____

Star patterns

Refresher and Practice

1. Work out how the first part of each pattern was drawn and complete the patterns.
2. Use colour to highlight the star patterns.

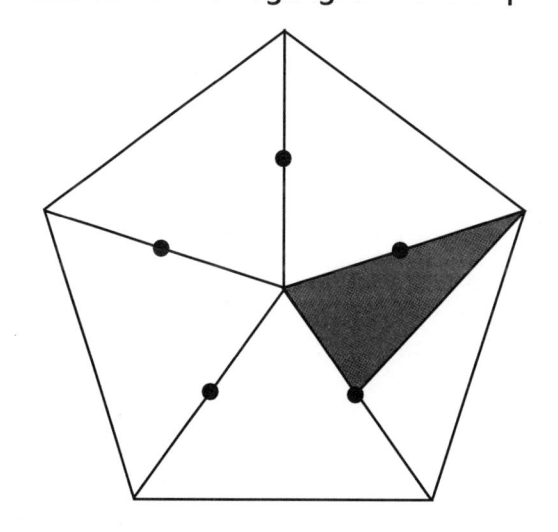

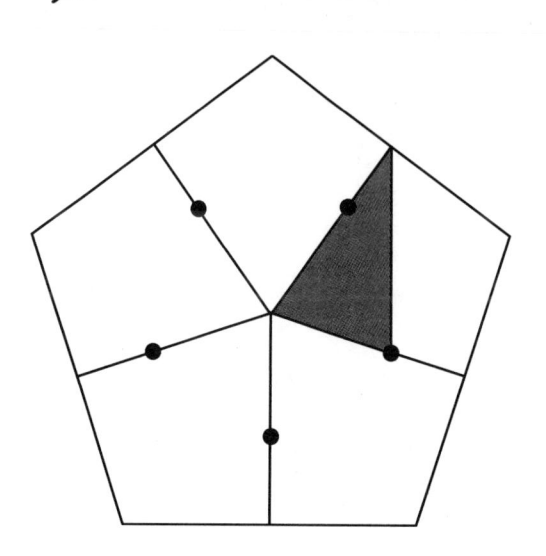

Practice

1. Continue and complete each pattern.
2. Add colour to show their rotation.

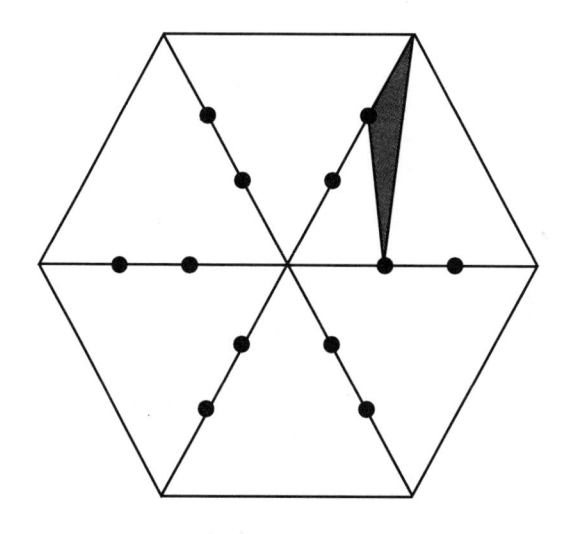

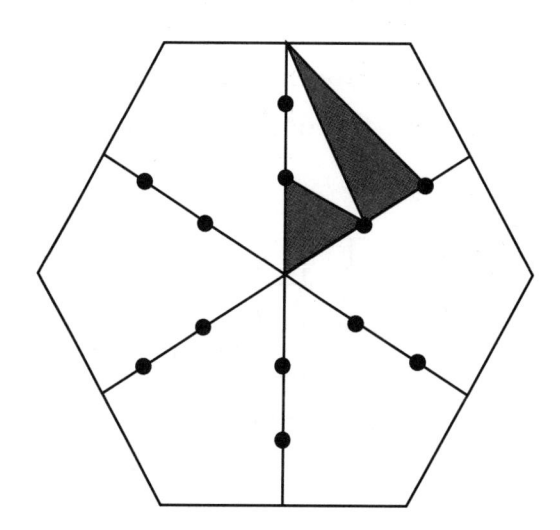

Collins Primary Maths © HarperCollins*Publishers* Ltd 2000

• Understand and use the formula in words "length × breadth" for the area of a rectangle   HCM 32

Name _____   Date _____

Finding the square units

Refresher and Practice

size of square
1 square millimetre 1 mm²
1 square centimetre 1 cm²
1 square metre 1 m²

1 Circle the size of square you think is best to measure these surfaces.

a a paperback book	b pop poster	c postcard
mm² cm² m²	mm² cm² m²	mm² cm² m²
d bed cover	e bedroom floor	f bedroom door
mm² cm² m²	mm² cm² m²	mm² cm² m²
g calculator key	h compact disc	i £1 coin
mm² cm² m²	mm² cm² m²	mm² cm² m²

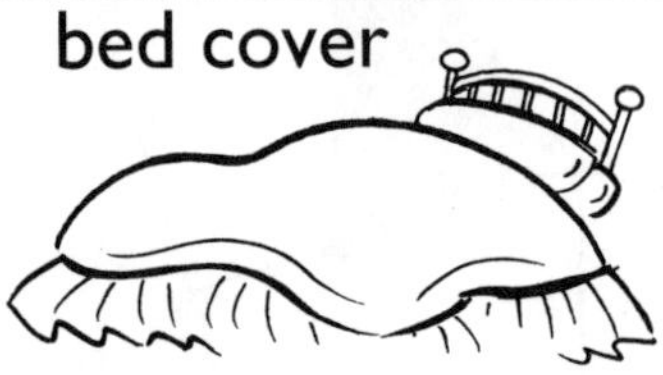

Practice

1 These windows have square panes of glass. Work out the area of glass in each window.

a 1 m × 1 m

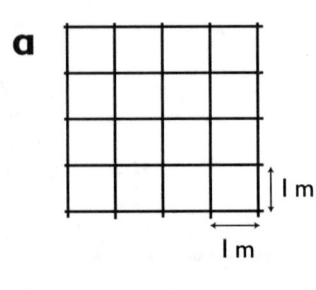

b 100 cm × 100 cm

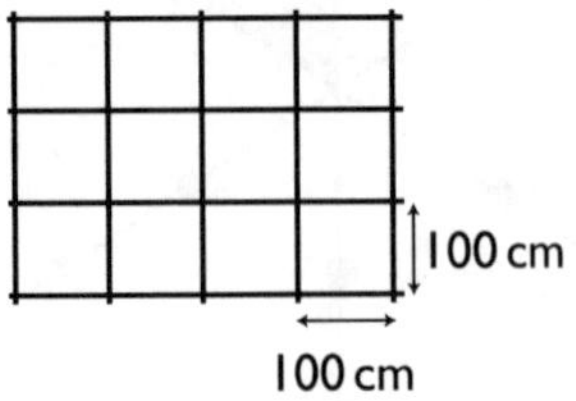

c 3 m × 6 m

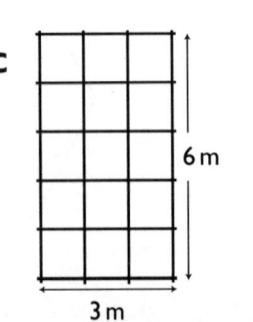

d 700 m × 200 m

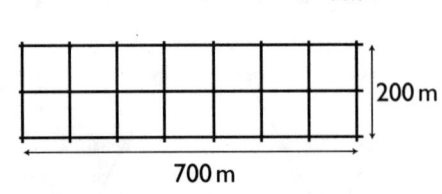

2 Which window will let in the most light? Answer: window _____

Collins Primary Maths © HarperCollinsPublishers Ltd 2000

● Use, read and write standard metric units of mass (kg, g) ...   HCM 33

Name _____   Date _____

Choosing chocolates

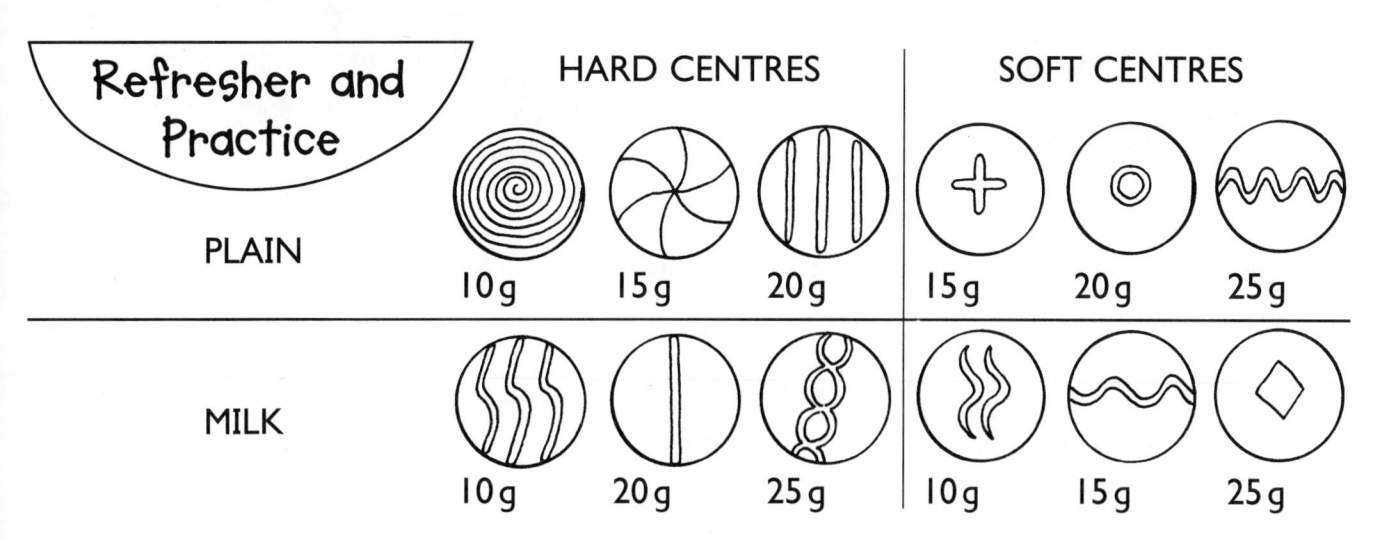

Refresher and Practice

	HARD CENTRES	SOFT CENTRES
PLAIN	10g 15g 20g	15g 20g 25g
MILK	10g 20g 25g	10g 15g 25g

1 Select and draw chocolates from each of the trays to fill your chocolate box.
2 Work out the total weight in grams of your selection.

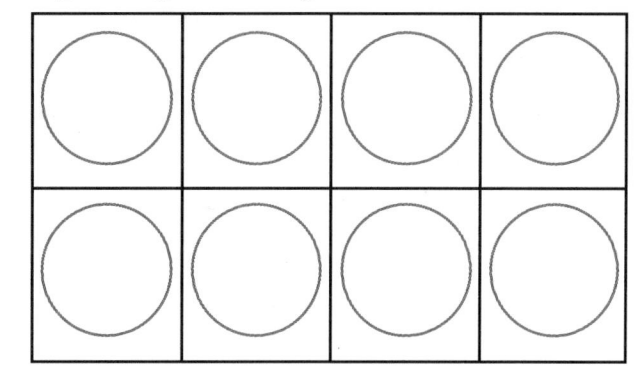

Total weight _____

Practice

1 Make a selection of 8 chocolates which will weigh 150g.
   You must have at least one chocolate from each tray.
   Write the weight of each chocolate in the grid below.

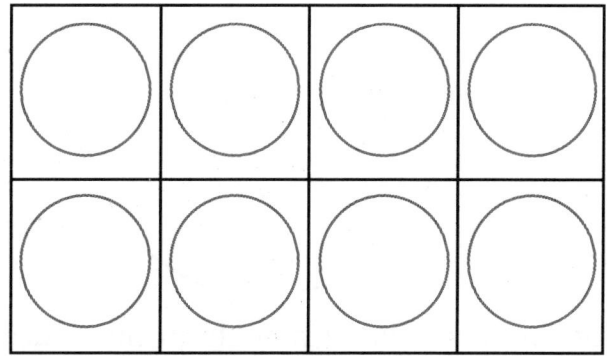

2 Work out the total weight of 8 chocolates you can select for:
   a the lightest box _____
   b the heaviest box _____

• Choose and use appropriate number operations to solve problems   HCM 34

Name _____ Date _____

Packaging weights

Refresher and Practice

1. Find 10 different packets, tins and jars.
2. Read the weight on the side of the container and write it in column 1.
3. Round the weight to the nearest 100 g and write your answer in column 2.

Container	Actual weight of container	Rounded to nearest 100g
Jar of mayonnaise	425 g	400 g
1		
2		
3		
4		
5		
6		
7		
8		
9		
10		

Practice

1. Write the actual weight of each container in the correct circle.

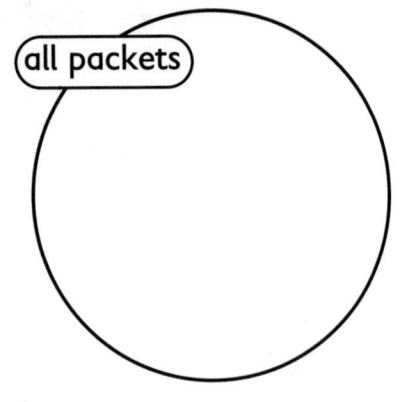

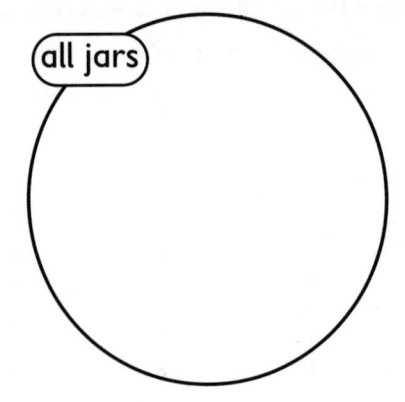

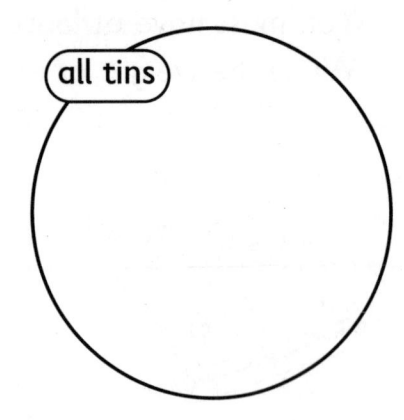

(all packets)   (all jars)   (all tins)

2. Round the weight of containers in each circle to the nearest 100 g.
   packets _____   jars _____   tins _____

3. Find the difference in weight between the heaviest and lightest set. _____

Collins Primary Maths © HarperCollinsPublishers Ltd 2000

● Solve a problem by representing and interpreting data in tables, charts, graphs and diagrams　　HCM 35

Name _____　Date _____

Pencil pack graphs

Refresher

1 Copy and complete the table of the prices.

£5 £6 £9 £3 £16 £13 £12

Number of pencils	Cost (£)

2 a How much does one pencil cost? ☐

   b How much do 3 pencils cost? ☐

   c Which is better value? Why? _____

Practice

1 Draw a line graph to show the prices of the pencil packs.

2 Gavin bought 10 pencils.

   a How much did he pay? ☐

   b How much does each pencil cost? ☐

3 Lucy bought one pencil to write some letters. She bought two more the next day.

   a How much did she spend altogether? ☐

   b Nancy could have bought all 3 pencils at once. How much would she have saved? ☐

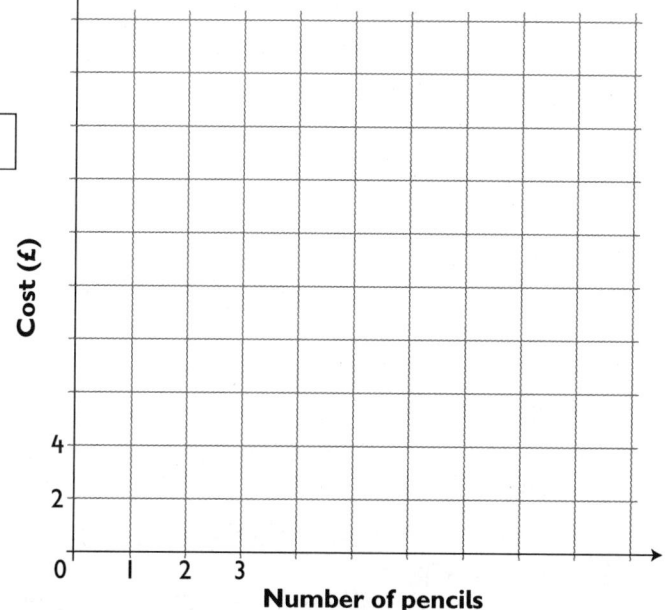

Cost of pencils

Cost (£)

0　1　2　3

Number of pencils

Collins Primary Maths © HarperCollinsPublishers Ltd 2000

● Add or subtract the nearest multiple of 10 or 100, then adjust

HCM 36

Name _____ Date _____

Near multiples magic

Refresher

	Calculations	How I worked it out.
1	138 + 41 =	138 + 40 + 1 =
2	152 + 31 =	
3	142 − 59 =	
4	161 − 29 =	
5	175 − 79 =	
6	184 + 89 =	
7	196 + 21 =	
8	205 − 39 =	

Practice

	Calculations	How I worked it out.
1	167 + 102 =	
2	238 + 198 =	
3	299 − 259 =	
4	364 − 301 =	
5	372 − 202 =	
6	483 + 399 =	
7	491 + 298 =	
8	573 − 398 =	

● Derive quickly or continue to derive quickly decimals that total 1 or 10   HCM 37

Name _____ Date _____

Decimal tens game

● You can play in pairs or on your own. First, cut out the cards and shuffle them.

● Place the cards face down on the table.

● Turn over two cards. If they equal 10, keep them. If they, do not put them back in the same place.

● If you are playing on your own, continue until you have all the pairs. If you are playing with a partner, take turns to choose cards until they are all taken. The player with the most pairs is the winner.

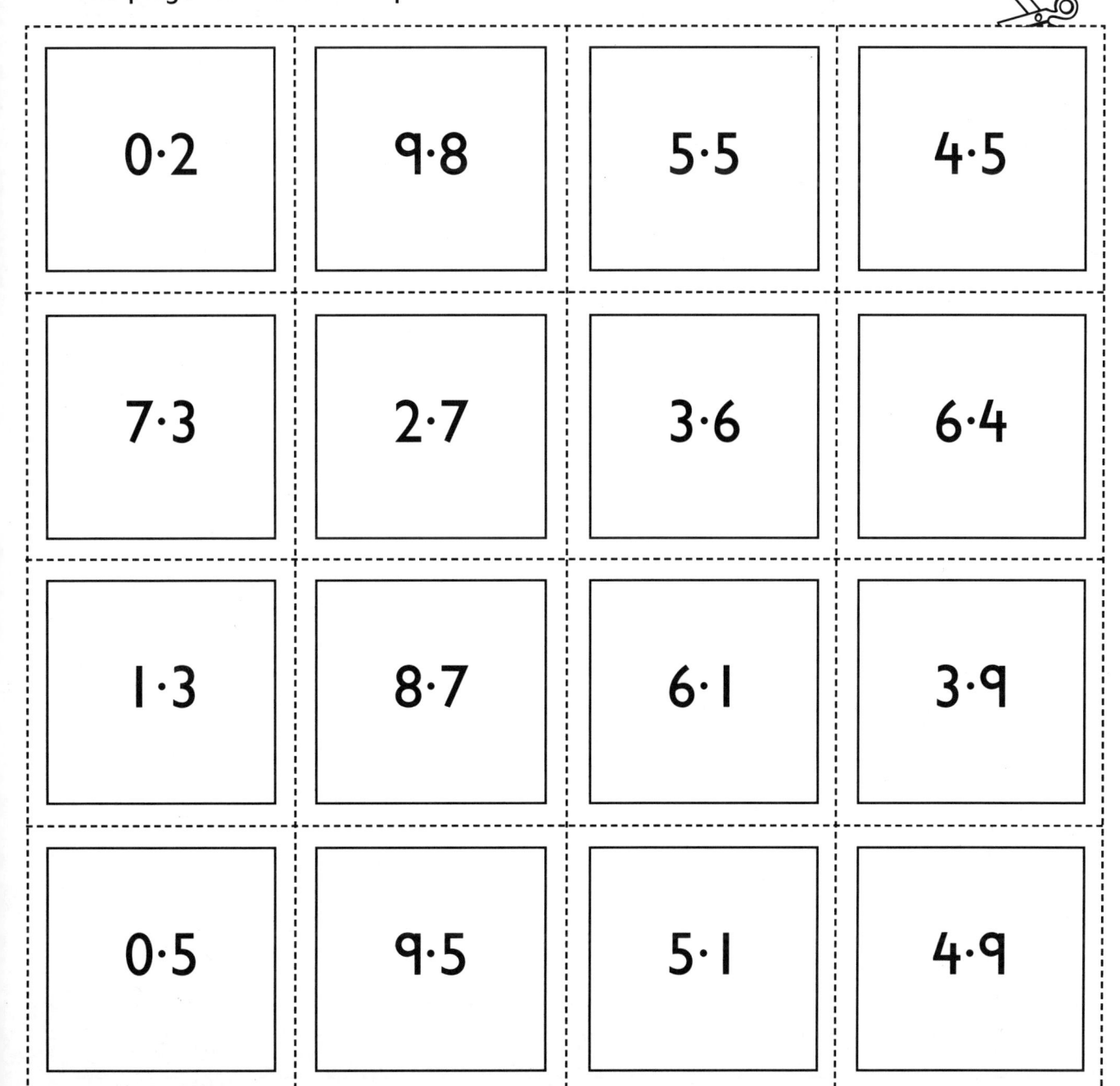

0·2	9·8	5·5	4·5
7·3	2·7	3·6	6·4
1·3	8·7	6·1	3·9
0·5	9·5	5·1	4·9

Collins Primary Maths © HarperCollinsPublishers Ltd 2000

HCM 38

● Extend written methods to addition of a pair of decimal fractions ...

Name _____ Date _____

Shopping decimals

Refresher

Ten customers each buys 2 items. Work out what each customer might have spent.

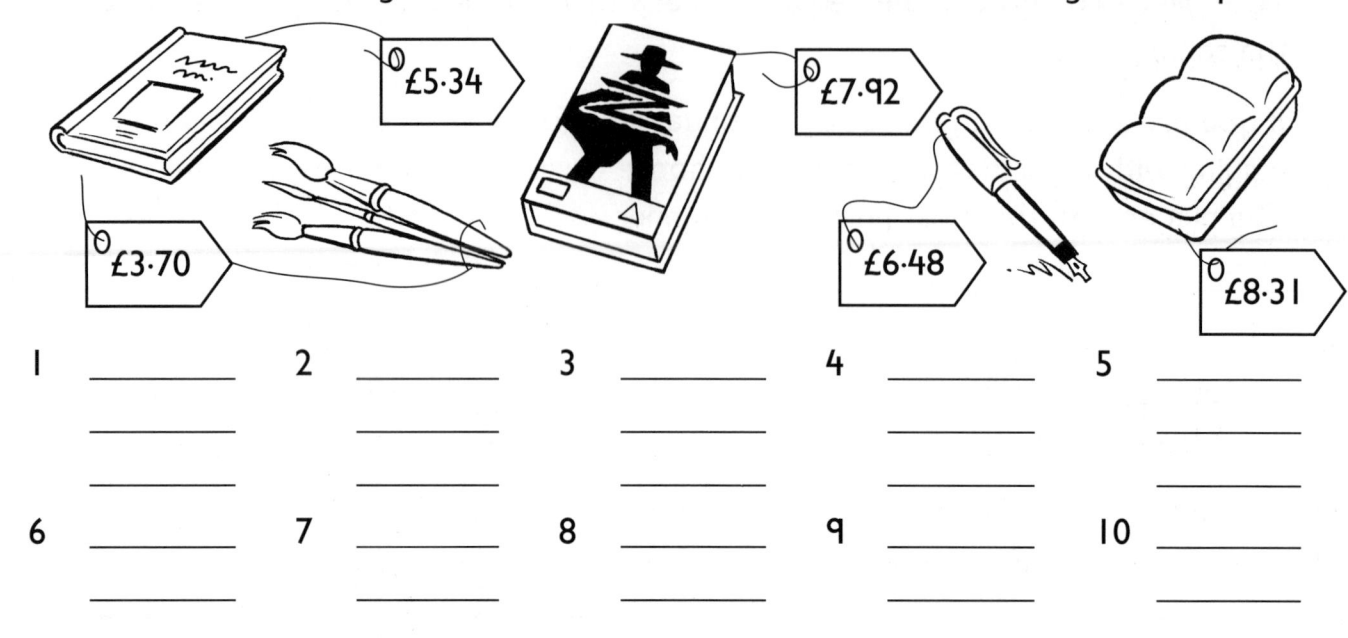

£5·34   £7·92
£3·70   £6·48   £8·31

1 _____   2 _____   3 _____   4 _____   5 _____

6 _____   7 _____   8 _____   9 _____   10 _____

Practice

Ten customers each buys 2 items. Work out what each person might have spent.

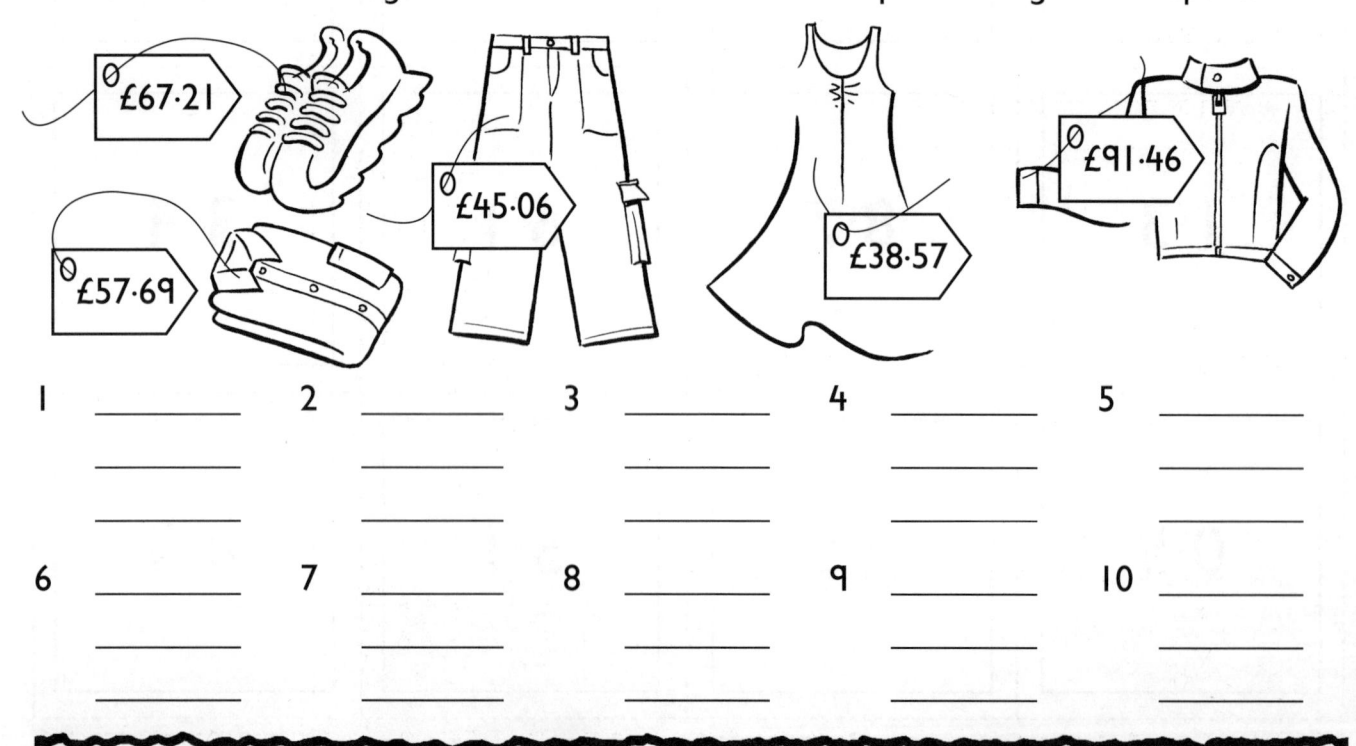

£67·21   £91·46
£57·69   £45·06   £38·57

1 _____   2 _____   3 _____   4 _____   5 _____

6 _____   7 _____   8 _____   9 _____   10 _____

Collins Primary Maths © HarperCollinsPublishers Ltd 2000

• Use addition and subtraction to solve simple word problems based on "real life" or money   HCM 39

Name _____ Date _____

Park problems

Refresher

working out

1. In a week, 1265 children played on the swings and 2873 on the slide. How many children used them altogether?

2. One family spent £6·15 on ice creams and another spent £4·26. How much was spent by the two families?

3. The length of one path is 6·23 km, and the other is 3·48 km. What is the total length of the paths?

4. One boy had £4·38. He lost £1·85. How much does he have left?

Practice

1. One week, 20 876 people went to the park. 1284 brought dogs with them. How many did not bring dogs?

2. Two joggers came into the park. One jogged 6·84 km and the other 8·36 km. What is the total distance jogged?

3. On Sunday, the ice-cream seller took £37·94 in the morning and £48·73 in the afternoon. How much did he take that day?

4. On a sunny day 2682 adults, 3727 children and 1375 dogs visit the park. How many visitors are there altogether?

Collins Primary Maths © HarperCollinsPublishers Ltd 2000

● Recognise and extend number sequences ... HCM 40

Name _____ Date _____

Look out for 25s

Refresher

1 Colour the numbers that are multiples of 25.

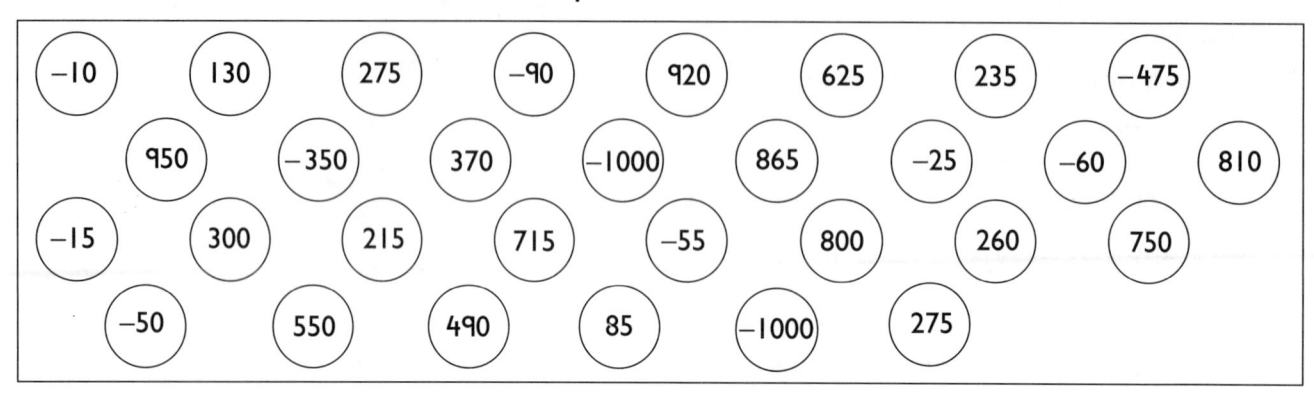

−10, 130, 275, −90, 920, 625, 235, −475, 950, −350, 370, −1000, 865, −25, −60, 810, −15, 300, 215, 715, −55, 800, 260, 750, −50, 550, 490, 85, −1000, 275

2 For each number line, write the number indicated by the boxes.

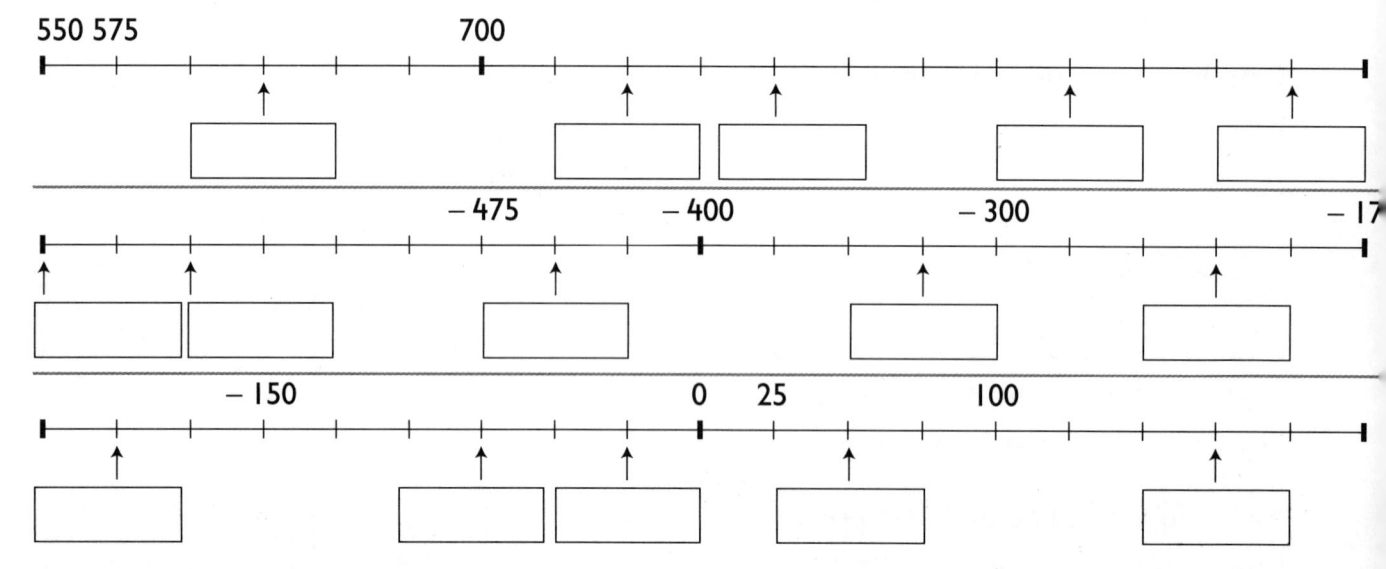

550 575   700

−475   −400   −300   −17

−150   0   25   100

Practice

1 Write the multiple of 25 that is:

a before 1000 →
b 75 more than −425 →
c after 725 →
d 100 more than −1000 →
e 25 less than −500 →
f 50 more than −950 →
g 25 more than −650 →
h 50 less than −325 →
i 75 less than 725 →
j 100 less than −475 →

Collins Primary Maths © HarperCollinsPublishers Ltd 2000

● Recognise multiples of 6, 7, 8, 9 up to the 10th multiple   HCM 41

Name _____ Date _____

Making many multiples

Refresher

Write the first 10 multiples of each of the numbers below.

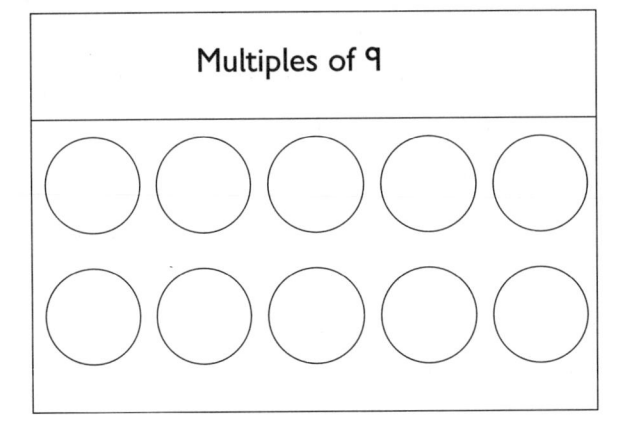

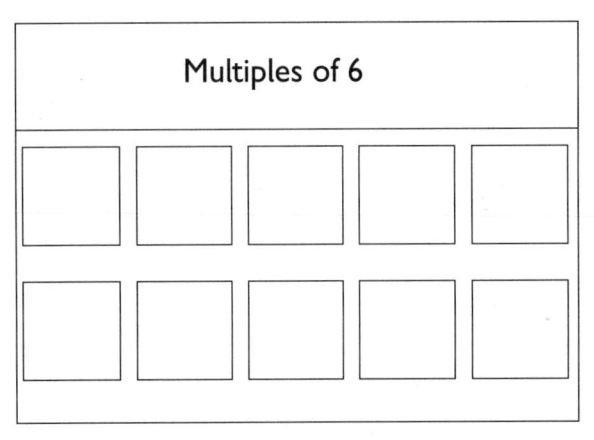

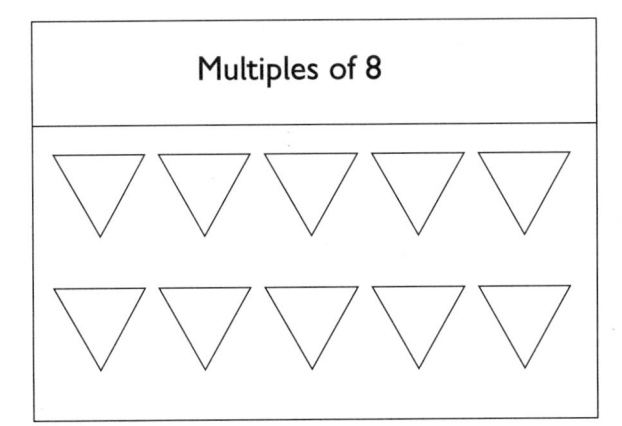

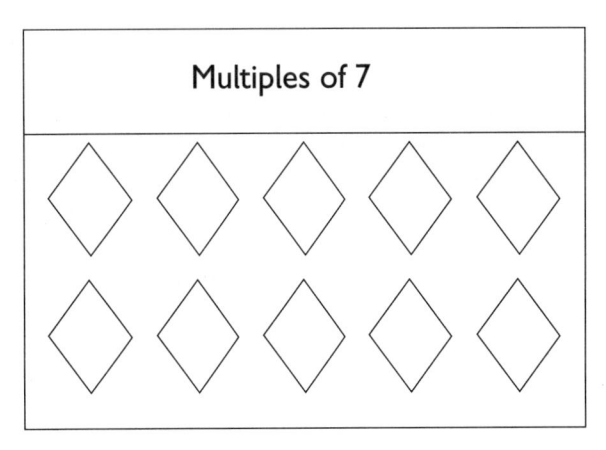

| Multiples of 9 | Multiples of 6 |
| Multiples of 8 | Multiples of 7 |

Practice

Look at the numbers you have written above.

a Find the common multiples of 9 and 7 _____

b Find the common multiples of 6 and 8 _____

c Find the common multiples of 6 and 9 _____

d Find the common multiples of 7 and 8 _____

e Find the common multiples of 7 and 6 _____

f Find the common multiples of 9 and 8 _____

Collins Primary Maths © HarperCollinsPublishers Ltd 2000

● Use the vocabulary of estimation and approximation   HCM 42

Name _____   Date _____

Estimates, estimates

Refresher

1. Estimate how many drinks you have in a week.

   About [ ] in a day.

   [ ] × 7 = about [ ] in a week.

2. Estimate how many bags of crisps you eat in a year.

   About [ ] in a week.

   [ ] × 52 = about [ ] in a year.

3. Estimate how many children are in Years 3, 4, 5 and 6.

   About [ ] in a year.

   [ ] × 4 = about [ ] in years 3, 4, 5 and 6.

Practice

1. Draw a line to show where to cut the rope.

   Example: $\frac{1}{4}$

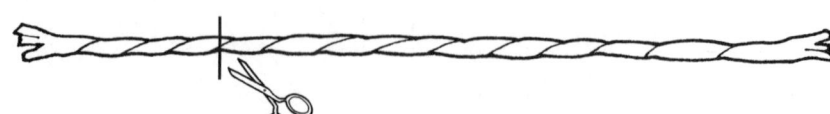

   a $\frac{1}{5}$

   b $\frac{2}{3}$

   c $\frac{9}{10}$

   d $\frac{2}{6}$

2. Estimate how many slices of bread your family eat in a year.

   About [ ] in a week.

   [ ] × 52 = about [ ] in a year.

HCM 43

Name _____ Date _____

Multiplication and division facts

Refresher

$+$ $-$ $\times$ $\div$

Write in the missing signs.

1 a 6 ___ 7 = 42   e 5 ___ 4 = 20   2 a 4 ___ 7 = 11   e 8 ___ 3 = 24
   b 6 ___ 7 = 13   f 24 ___ 3 = 8   b 20 ___ 3 = 17 f 8 ___ 4 = 2
   c 18 ___ 9 = 9   g 25 ___ 5 = 5   c 32 ___ 4 = 8   g 12 ___ 5 = 17
   d 18 ___ 6 = 3   h 7 ___ 7 = 0   d 32 ___ 4 = 28 h 12 ___ 4 = 3

Practice

Write a multiplication or division calculation for each of the following.
Then work out the answer.

		Calculation	Answer
1	What is the product of 8 and 7?		
2	What is 9 times itself?		
3	There are 72 biscuits. Each packet contains 9 biscuits. How many packets?		
4	How many times does 4 go into 84?		
5	What are 5 lots of 12?		
6	What is the quotient of 24 and 6?		
7	A baker uses 7 dozen eggs per day. How many eggs is this?		
8	There are 52 playing cards in a "deck". Split the deck between 4 players. How many cards do they each get?		
9	John has 6 blue marbles and 7 times as many green marbles. How many marbles does he have altogether?		
10	What is 49 divided by 7?		

Collins Primary Maths © HarperCollinsPublishers Ltd 2000

• Use known facts and place value to multiply and divide mentally   HCM 44

Name _____   Date _____

Multiplication and division

Refresher

Sort these calculations into groups as shown.

200 × 10	5000 ÷ 10	350 ÷ 2	94 × 5
450 × 2	65 × 6	40 × 100	680 ÷ 2
7000 ÷ 100	300 × 10	38 × 3	420 ÷ 2
56 × 4	365 × 2	485 × 2	29 × 7
9000 ÷ 100	87 × 9	760 ÷ 2	77 × 6

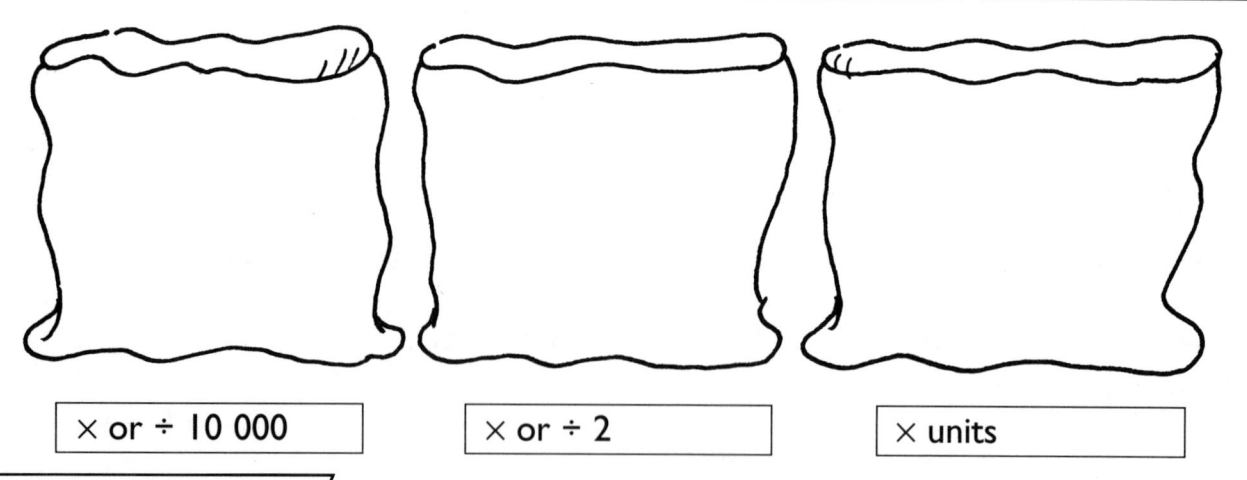

× or ÷ 10 000   × or ÷ 2   × units

Practice

Work the answers out to each of the calculations above in your head.
Write the answers in the right places below.

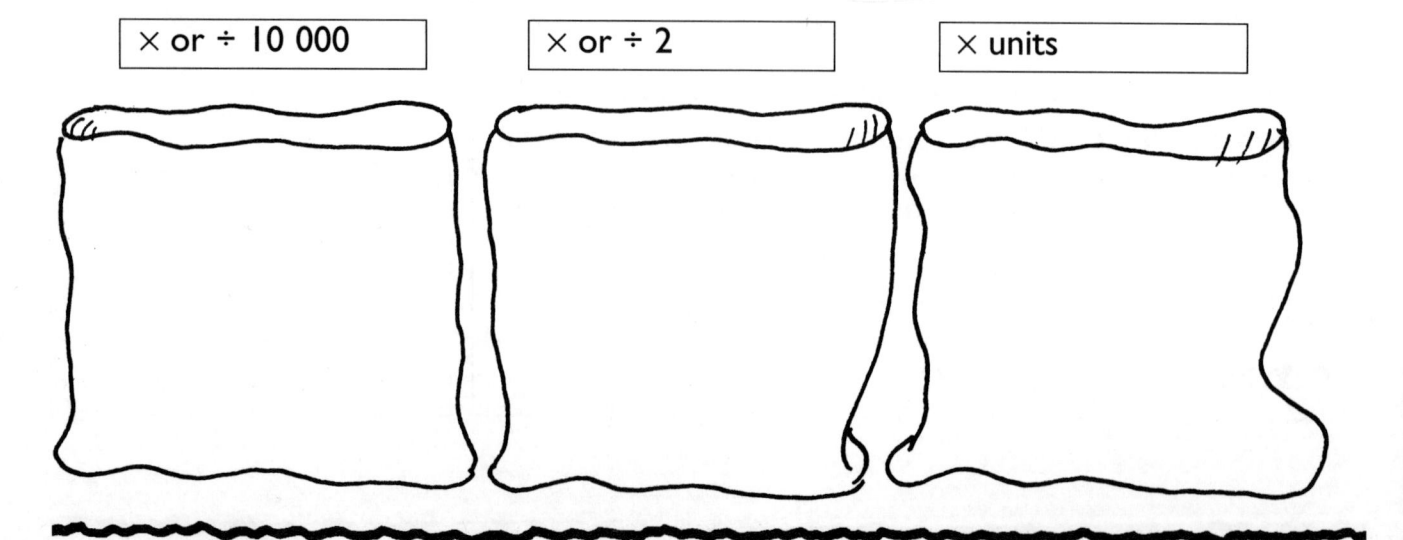

× or ÷ 10 000   × or ÷ 2   × units

● Use known facts and place value ... HCM 45

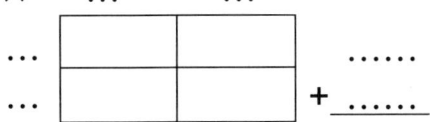

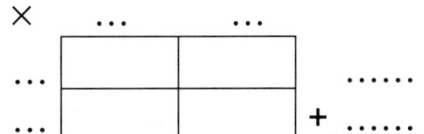

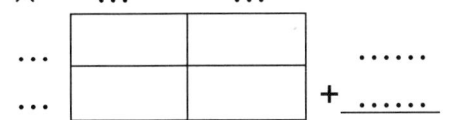

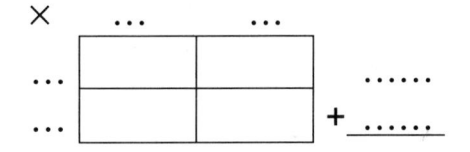

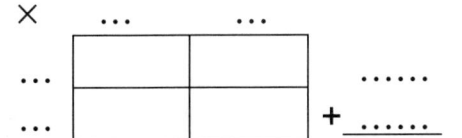

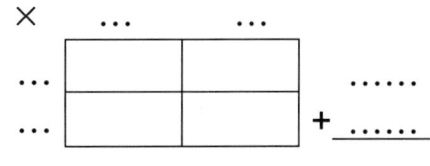

Name _____ Date _____

Multiplication methods

Refresher

Approximate the answer to each calculation.

a 19×38 ∘○○ $20 \times 40 = 800$

b 27×33 ∘○○

c 44×38 ∘○○

d 39×55 ∘○○

e 48×56 ∘○○

f 28×63 ∘○○

g 24×43 ∘○○

h 34×72 ∘○○

Practice

For each of the calculations above, use the grid method to work out the answer.

a 19×38

×	10	9
30		
8		

b

c

d

e

f

g

h

Collins Primary Maths © HarperCollinsPublishers Ltd 2000

● Know by heart all multiplication facts up to 10 × 10   HCM 46

Name _____   Date _____

More multiplication methods

Refresher

Approximate the answer to each calculation.

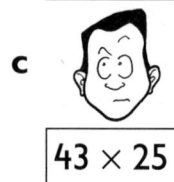

a 22 × 33

b 31 × 27

c 43 × 25

d 55 × 37

e 24 × 16

f 32 × 19

Practice

For each calculation above, work out the answer using the standard method of recording. Check your answer is close to your approximation.

a
```
        22
      × 33
      ____
(22 × 30)
(22 × 3)  ____
          ____
```

b
```
        31
      × 27
      ____
(31 × 20)
(31 × 7)  ____
          ____
```

c
```
        43
      × 25
      ____
          ____
          ____
```

d
```
        55
      × 37
      ____
          ____
          ____
```

e
```
        24
      × 16
      ____
          ____
          ____
```

f
```
        32
      × 19
      ____
          ____
          ____
```

Collins Primary Maths © HarperCollinsPublishers Ltd 2000

● Order a set of numbers or measurements with the same number of decimal places   HCM 47

Name _____   Date _____

Decimal jumps

Refresher

Label the jumps the frogs have made.

Stones: 1.3, 1.6, 2, 2.5, 2.7, 3, 3.4, 3.8, 4, 4.2, 4.7

Practice

Label the jumps the frogs have made.

Stones: 2.35, 2.39, 4.42, 4.47, 4.50, 4.58, 4.60, 4.63, 4.67, 4.72, 4.79

Collins Primary Maths © HarperCollinsPublishers Ltd 2000

● Relate fractions to their decimal representations   HCM 48

Name _____   Date _____

Fraction and decimal dominoes

Cut out the dominoes and complete the domino circle matching the fractions to the equivalent decimal.

Refresher

| $\frac{3}{4}$ | 0.5 |

| $\frac{2}{10}$ | 0.75 |

| $\frac{1}{2}$ | 0.6 |

| 0.4 | $\frac{1}{10}$ |

| 0.25 | $\frac{4}{10}$ |

| 0.1 | $\frac{6}{10}$ |

| $\frac{1}{4}$ | 0.8 |

| $\frac{8}{10}$ | 0.2 |

Practice

| 0.12 | $\frac{2}{5}$ |

| $\frac{96}{100}$ | 0.25 |

| $\frac{1}{5}$ | 0.02 |

| $\frac{1}{4}$ | 0.2 |

| $\frac{2}{100}$ | 0.68 |

| 0.96 | $\frac{3}{4}$ |

| $\frac{68}{100}$ | 0.4 |

| 0.75 | $\frac{12}{100}$ |

Collins Primary Maths © HarperCollinsPublishers Ltd 2000

● To begin to understand percentage as the number of parts in every 100   HCM 49

Name _____   Date _____

Four in a row

For 2 players

How to play
- Decide which version of the game you are going to play.
- Each person takes a colour pen.
- Take it in turns to throw the die.
- See what percent of the grid you can colour in by looking at the table at the bottom of the page. Colour your squares.
- Keep going until the grid is completely coloured.
- Work out your total percentage.
  The person with the highest percent is the winner.

You need
- two coloured felt-tip pens
- a die

Refresher

Die	1	2	3	4	5	6
%	25%	10%	10%	5%	20%	20%

Practice

Die	1	2	3	4	5	6
%	8%	17%	1%	11%	15%	21%

Collins Primary Maths © HarperCollinsPublishers Ltd 2000

● Solve simple problems involving ratio and proportion   HCM 50

Name _____ Date _____

How many?

Refresher

1. Two brothers have 20 stickers to share out between them.
   The older brother decides for every one his brother has, he will have three.
   Complete the table to work out how many stickers they both get.
   Answer _____

Older brother	Younger brother
1	3

2. To make a litre of green paint you need 2 tins of blue paint for every 3 tins of yellow paint.
   How many tins do I need to make 5 litres of paint?
   Complete the table to help you work it out.
   Answer _____

Blue	Yellow	Amount
2	3	1 litre

Practice

1. Chicken must be cooked 50 minutes for every kg.
   How long does it take to cook a 4 kg chicken?
   Complete the table to help you work it out.
   Answer _____

Cooking time	Chicken
50 minutes	1 kg

2. To make up the orange squash, you need 10 ml of squash for every 100 ml of water.
   I have 50 ml of squash, so how much can I make up?
   Complete the table to help you work it out.
   Answer _____

   If I make up a litre, how much squash will I need? _____

Squash	Water
10 ml	100 ml

● Calculate the range of a set of data HCM 51

Name _____ Date _____

Ranges

Refresher

1 Calculate the range of drill sizes.

a) 2mm, 3mm, 7mm, 9mm

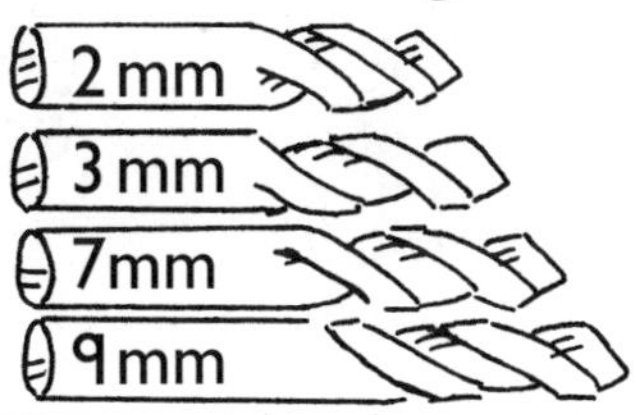

Range _____

b) 12mm, 20mm, 25mm, 27mm, 38mm

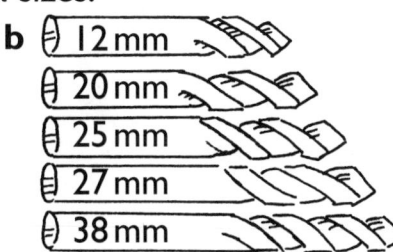

Range _____

c) 1·5mm, 2mm, 3·5mm, 5·5mm

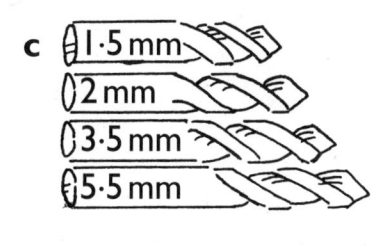

Range _____

2 a What is the smallest drill size? _____

b What is the largest drill size? _____

(24mm, 8mm, 10·5mm, 15mm, 25mm, 9·5mm)

Practice

1 Calculate the range of staple sizes for each brand.

a Clampit: No 29, No 38, No 16, No 42

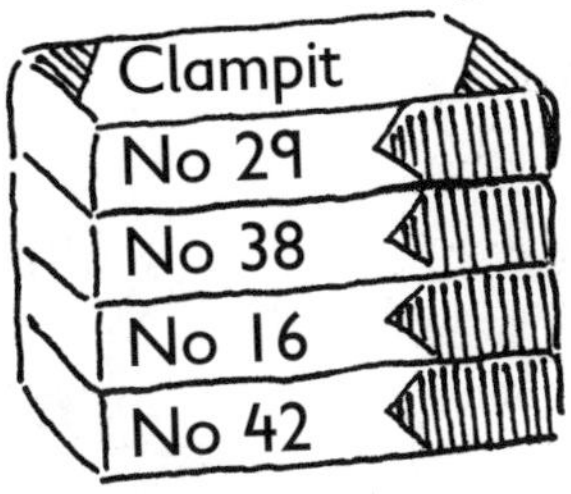

Range _____

b Holdfast: No 25, No 7, No 19, No 28

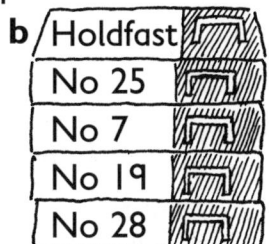

Range _____

c Gripper: No 15, No 27, No 4, No 11, No 19

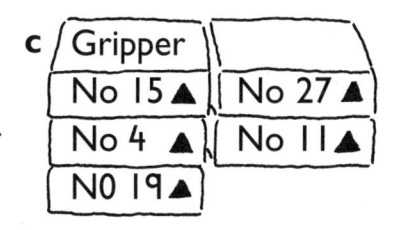

Range _____

2 Which brand has the smallest range of sizes? _____

3 Calculate the range of screw lengths each shop sells.

a Ted's DIY SCREWS: 3·5cm, 5·5cm, 1·5cm, 6cm

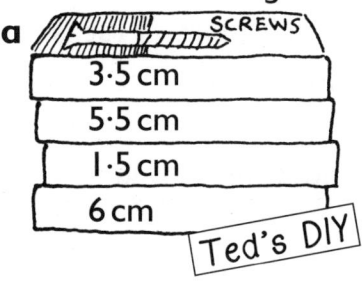

Range _____

b Timber World: 8cm, 12cm, 7cm, 10cm

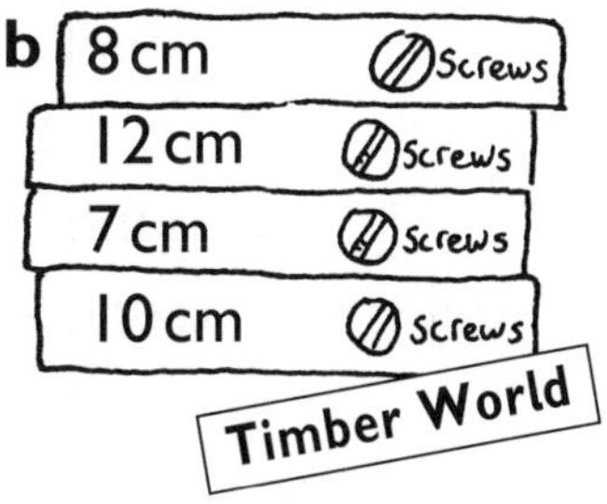

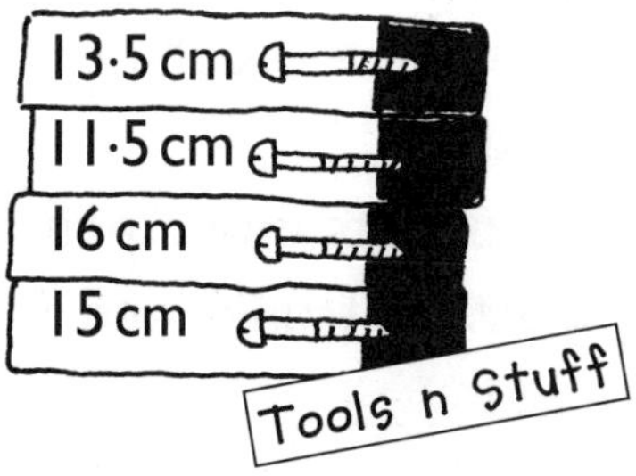

Range _____

c Tools n Stuff: 13·5cm, 11·5cm, 16cm, 15cm

Range _____

4 Which shop has the widest range of screws for sale? _____

● Develop calulator skills and use a calculator effectively   HCM 52

Name _____ Date _____

Sports costs

Refresher

You need:
● a calculator

Tennis racket £28
Table tennis bat £17
Hockey stick £41
Table tennis ball 72p
Shuttlecock 94p
Wristband 58p

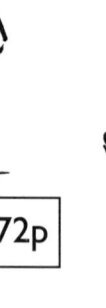

Calculate the cost in £ and p. Show your working.

a 3 rackets and bat _____
b 4 bats and 2 hockey sticks _____
c 5 rackets, a bat and a hockey stick _____
d 6 balls and 2 shuttlecocks _____

e 10 balls and 3 wristbands _____
f 2 wristbands and 8 shuttlecocks _____
g 3 balls, 4 wristbands and 6 shuttlecocks _____

Practice

1

Football boots £34
Tracksuit £19
Swimming trunks £7·26
Boot laces 55p
Headband 84p

Use your calculator to find the total cost in £ and p. Show your working.

a 3 pairs of football boots and a tracksuit _____
b 5 tracksuits and a pair of trunks _____
c 2 pairs of trunks and 3 pairs of football boots _____

d 2 headbands and 2 pairs of laces _____
e A pair of trunks and 3 headbands _____
f 2 tracksuits and 3 pairs of laces _____

2 a How much more does a pair of boots cost than a pair of trunks?
   _____
   b How much more does a pair of trunks cost than a headband?
   _____

● Complete symmetrical patterns with two lines of symmetry at right angles   HCM 53

Name _____   Date _____

Four-square designs

Refresher

Each pattern has 2 lines of symmetry.
Complete these patterns.

Example
One sector   Complete pattern

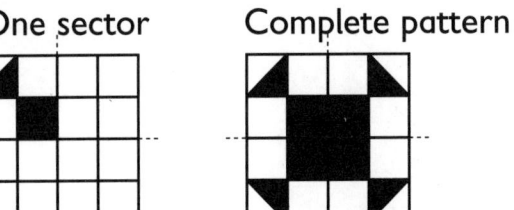

Lines of symmetry

a   b 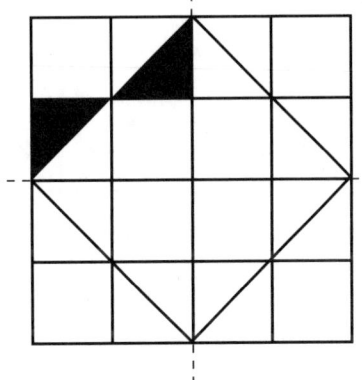   c

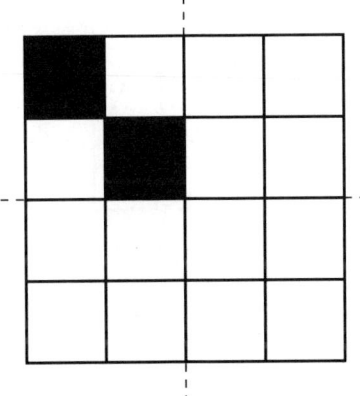

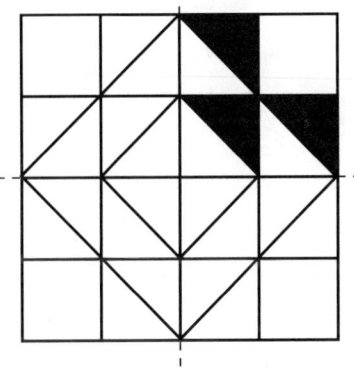

d 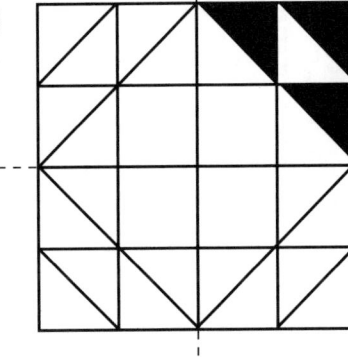   e 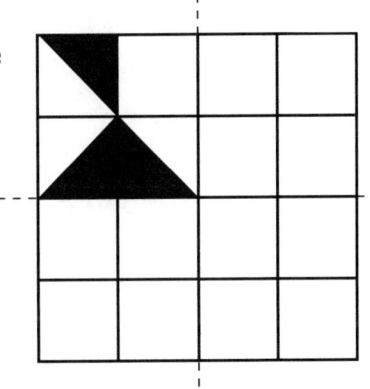   f

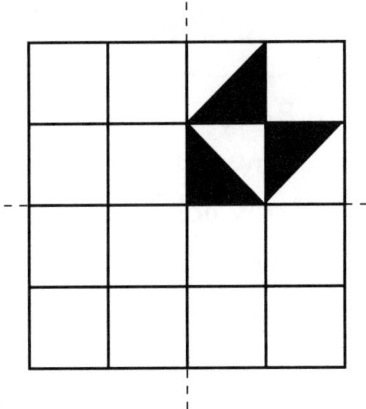

Practice

Use two colours.
Make 3 different patterns with 2 axes of symmetry.

a   b 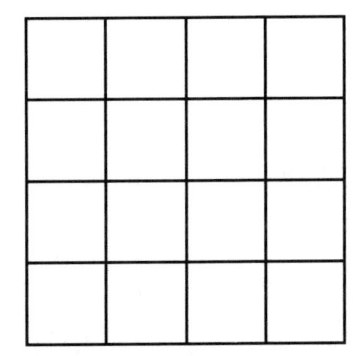   c

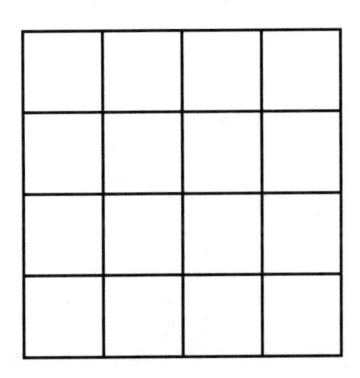

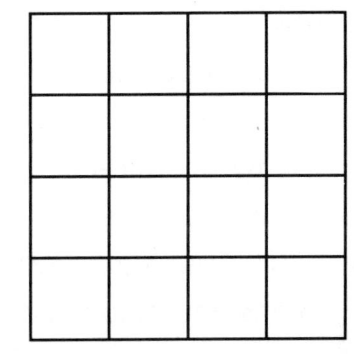

Collins Primary Maths © HarperCollins*Publishers* Ltd 2000

● Complete symmetrical patterns with two lines of symmetry at right angles

HCM 54

Name _____ Date _____

Making a Rangoli pattern

How to make a Rangoli pattern.

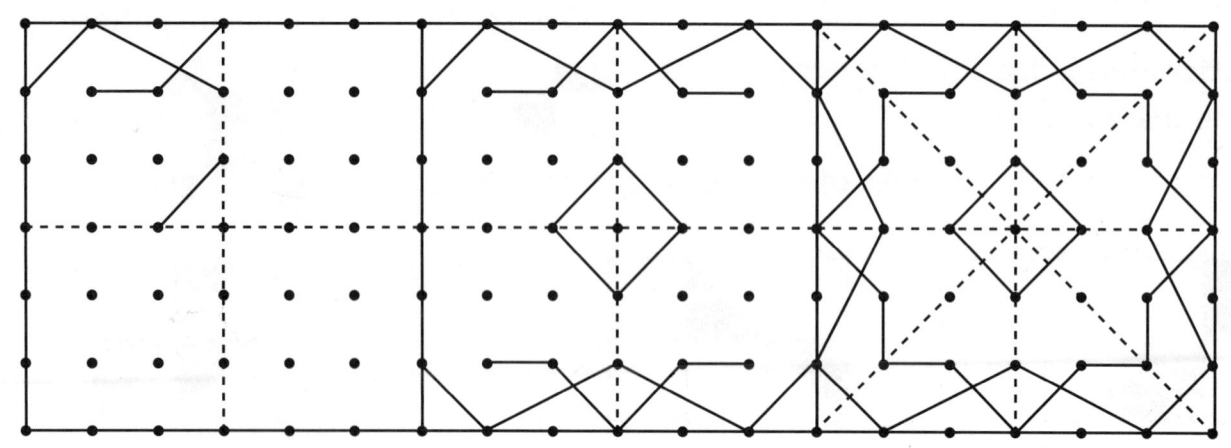

Draw 5 lines that do not pass through another point.

Reflect the lines in the horizontal and vertical axes.

Now reflect the lines in both diagonal axes.

Refresher

Make a Rangoli pattern in this square.
    a Draw in the axes of symmetry.
       Draw lightly in pencil, so they can be rubbed out later.
    b Colour your pattern to show its symmetry.

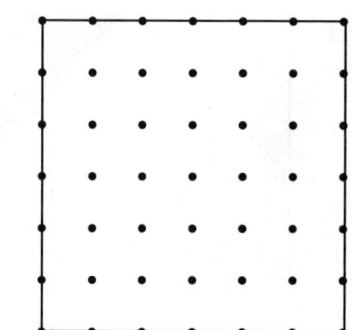

Practice

Make your own Rangoli pattern.
    a Draw a Rangoli pattern in the first square.
    b Either:
       Repeat your Rangoli pattern in the other 3 squares, and see what happens!
       Or:
       Draw a different Rangoli pattern in each square.
    c Work out symmetrical colouring plans and colour your designs.

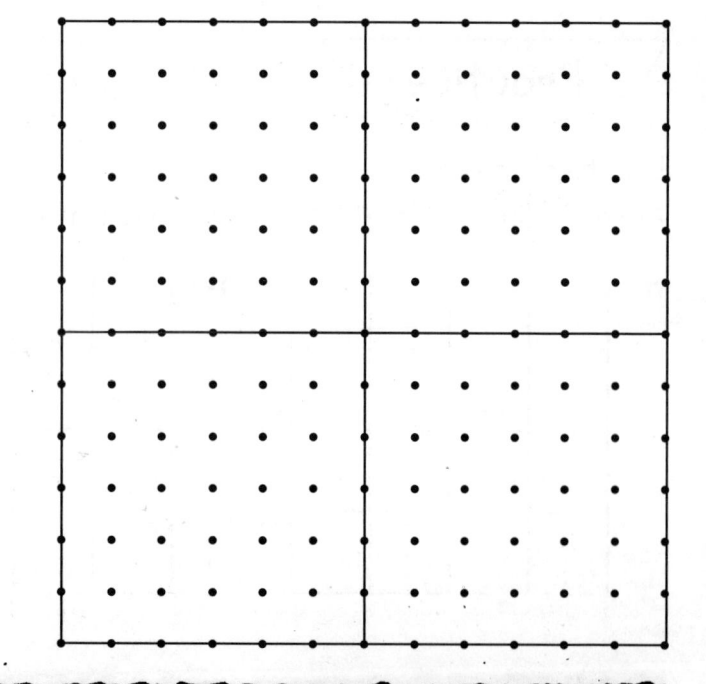

Collins Primary Maths © HarperCollins*Publishers* Ltd 2000

● Recognise where a shape will be after a translation   HCM 55

Name _____   Date _____

Translation patterns

Refresher

Each square is one unit.

1 In the top row, translate the octagon 2 units to the left, then 2 units to the right.

2 Repeat, as above for the second row.

3 Use 3 colours: one for each shape and one for the space between.

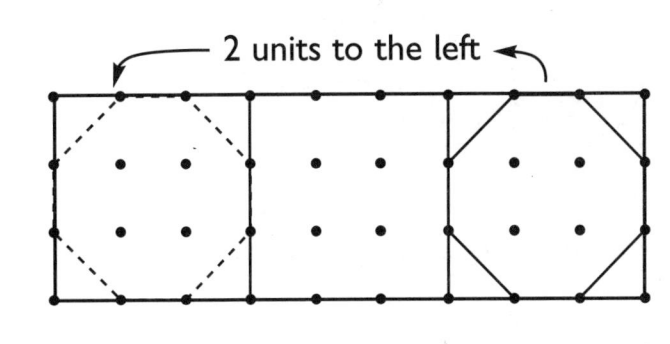

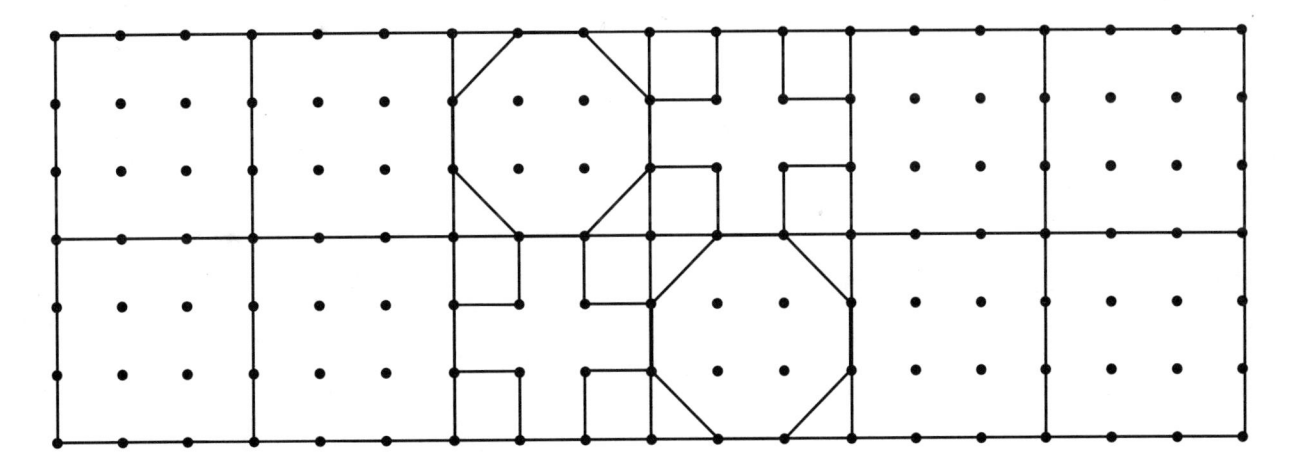

Practice

1 For each row, translate the hexagon 2 units to the left, then 2 units to the right.

2 Repeat, as above for the other polygon.

3 Use 3 colours to highlight your translation pattern.

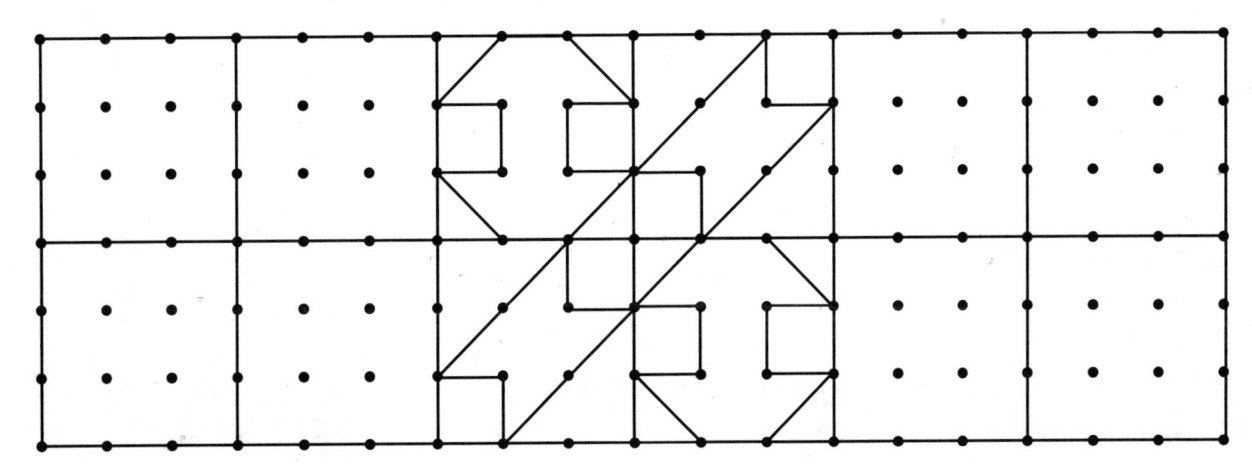

Collins Primary Maths © HarperCollins*Publishers* Ltd 2000

● Know and use the relationships between units of time HCM 56

Name _____ Date _____

My birthday

> Remember to count the extra day in February when it is a leap year.

Refresher

This is how David worked out the day of the week on which his younger brother was born.

Copy and complete your details here.

1 Date of birth.
   22nd June 1998

2 Is the year a leap year?
   No

3 Number of days from
   1st January to 22nd June
   173
   Jan Feb Mar Apr May Jun
   31 + 28 + 31 + 30 + 31 + 22 = 173

4 Subtract 1 from year, divide by 4. Ignore any remainder.
   1998 − 1 = 1997
   1997 ÷ 4 = 499

5 Add together   number of days   173
                   year of birth   1998
                   answer to 4   + 499
                   total   2670

6 Divide 2670 by 7
   Remainder
   2670 ÷ 7 = 381 r 3
   3

7 Use the table of remainders:
   Fri Sat Sun Mon Tue Wed Thu
   0   1   2   3   4   5   6
   (Remainder of 3 = M) Monday

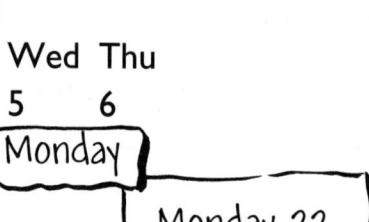

8 Day of birth
   Monday 22 June 1998

Practice

Ask someone in your family for their date of birth. Using the other side of this sheet, find out the day of the week on which they were born.

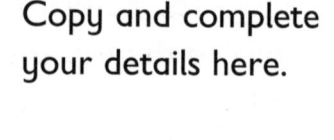

● Suggest suitable units and measuring equipment to estimate or measure capacity   HCM 57

Name _____ Date _____

Everyday estimating

Refresher

1. Find about 8 different bottles, jars or containers in your kitchen and bathroom.
2. Turn each container so that you cannot see the label for the number of millilitres.
3. For each item, write its name in column 1 and your estimate, in ml, in column 2.
4. Write the amount on the label in column 3.
5. Write the difference between your estimate and the amount on the label in column 4.

Container 1	Capacity in ml		
	Estimate 2	Measure on label 3	Difference 4
a			
b			
c			
d			
e			
f			
g			
h			

Practice

You need a 5 ml measure or a medicine spoon. Food items such as sauce, tomato ketchup, jam and marmalade are usually measured in grams.

1. Choose any one of the above items.
   Find a way to measure, in millilitres, either:
   ● how much jam you spread on a slice of bread, or:
   ● how much sauce or ketchup you use for a portion of chips or other food.
2. Write about what you found out. _____
   _____

● Derive quickly or continue to derive quickly decimals that total 1 and 10   HCM 58

Name _____ Date _____

Learn your facts!

Refresher — Learn the decimals that go together to equal 1.

1. Read the first column and try and remember the facts.
2. Cover the first column and work out the second column as quickly as you can. Mark your answers.
3. Cover the first and second columns and work out the third column. Try and beat your score.

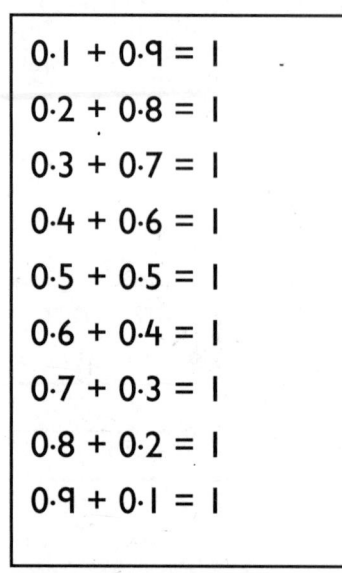

0·1 + 0·9 = 1	0·5 + ☐ = 1	0·1 + ☐ = 1
0·2 + 0·8 = 1	0·4 + ☐ = 1	0·8 + ☐ = 1
0·3 + 0·7 = 1	0·9 + ☐ = 1	0·4 + ☐ = 1
0·4 + 0·6 = 1	0·7 + ☐ = 1	0·7 + ☐ = 1
0·5 + 0·5 = 1	0·2 + ☐ = 1	0·2 + ☐ = 1
0·6 + 0·4 = 1	0·6 + ☐ = 1	0·6 + ☐ = 1
0·7 + 0·3 = 1	0·1 + ☐ = 1	0·3 + ☐ = 1
0·8 + 0·2 = 1	0·3 + ☐ = 1	0·5 + ☐ = 1
0·9 + 0·1 = 1	0·8 + ☐ = 1	0·9 + ☐ = 1

Practice — Learn the decimals that go together to equal 10.

1. Complete the first column as quickly as you can. Mark your answers.
2. Complete the other two columns. Each time try and beat your score.

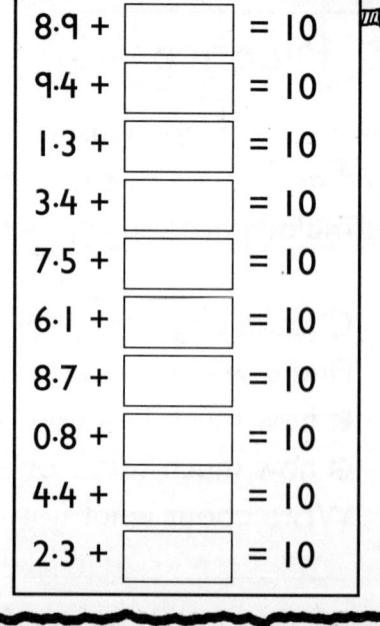

4·5 + ☐ = 10	1·5 + ☐ = 10	8·9 + ☐ = 10
2·3 + ☐ = 10	6·3 + ☐ = 10	9·4 + ☐ = 10
7·6 + ☐ = 10	7·5 + ☐ = 10	1·3 + ☐ = 10
4·2 + ☐ = 10	1·8 + ☐ = 10	3·4 + ☐ = 10
3·9 + ☐ = 10	4·9 + ☐ = 10	7·5 + ☐ = 10
8·5 + ☐ = 10	6·4 + ☐ = 10	6·1 + ☐ = 10
1·8 + ☐ = 10	7·8 + ☐ = 10	8·7 + ☐ = 10
0·4 + ☐ = 10	1·4 + ☐ = 10	0·8 + ☐ = 10
3·3 + ☐ = 10	0·8 + ☐ = 10	4·4 + ☐ = 10
7·9 + ☐ = 10	7·6 + ☐ = 10	2·3 + ☐ = 10

Collins Primary Maths © HarperCollinsPublishers Ltd 2000

HCM 59

Name _____ Date _____

Sum choice

Refresher

Choose numbers and make up 5 addition and 5 subtraction calculations.
Work them out using the vertical method.

| 6·47 | 2·71 | 5·03 | 3·81 | 7·85 | 2·35 | 4·23 | 2·12 | 8·24 | 9·26 |

5·03   8·34

Practice

Choose numbers and make up 5 addition and 5 subtraction calculations.
Work them out on the other side of this sheet, using the vertical method.

| 12·62 | 4·83 | 15·72 | 8·62 | 24·72 | 9·85 | 13·42 | 6·13 | 25·96 | 2·72 |

24·72   6·13

Collins Primary Maths © HarperCollinsPublishers Ltd 2000

● Find all the pairs of factors of any number up to 100 **HCM 60**

Name _____ Date _____

Flower factors

Refresher

Colour the factors for each number.

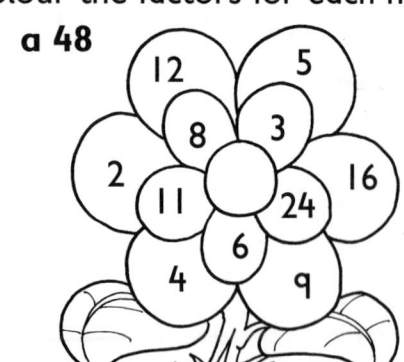

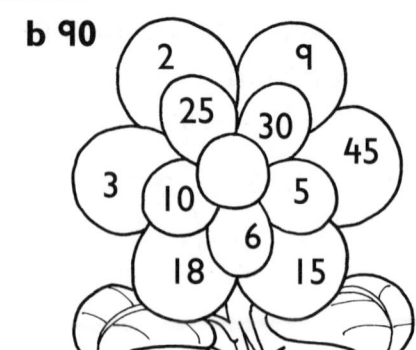

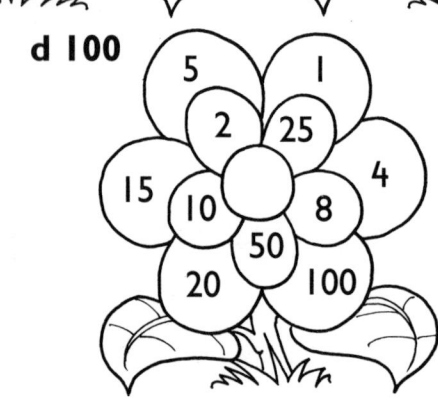

a 48 — petals: 12, 5, 3, 16, 24, 6, 9, 4, 11, 2, 8 (centre)

b 90 — petals: 2, 9, 30, 45, 5, 6, 15, 18, 10, 3, 25

c 36 — petals: 1, 2, 3, 16, 8, 36, 12, 6, 18, 9, 4

d 100 — petals: 5, 1, 25, 4, 8, 100, 20, 10, 15, 50, 2

e 56 — petals: 1, 14, 9, 4, 12, 7, 28, 56, 6, 2, 8

Practice

Write all the factors for each pair of numbers in order.
Circle the common factors for each pair.

a 12 → _____
   16 → _____

b 24 → _____
   32 → _____

c 18 → _____
   45 → _____

d 20 → _____
   36 → _____

e 64 → _____
   96 → _____

f 72 → _____
   85 → _____

Collins Primary Maths © HarperCollinsPublishers Ltd 2000